OKLAHOMA
A Story Through Her People

Photography by **James Larrick**
Text by **Bob Burke** and
Eric Dabney

In partnership with
Oklahoma Heritage Association Publishing,
a publication of the Oklahoma Hall of Fame

HPNbooks
A division of Lammert Incorporated
San Antonio, Texas

11200 Pine Street, Tulsa, Oklahoma 74116

918-878-6837 • www.NORDAM.com

First Edition

Copyright © 2015 HPNbooks

ISBN: 978-1-939300-84-3

Library of Congress Card Catalog Number: 2015941570

OKLAHOMA: A Story Through Her People

photographer:	James Larrick
authors:	Bob Burke, Eric Dabney
designer:	Glenda Tarazon Krouse
contributing writers for Oklahoma partners:	Garnette Bane, Eric Dabney, Joe Goodpasture, Marie Beth Jones
contributing writers for photography chapters:	Gini Moore Campbell, Lou Ann Murphy

HPNbooks

president:	Ron Lammert
project manager:	Lou Ann Murphy
administration:	Donna M. Mata, Melissa G. Quinn
book sales:	Dee Steidle
production:	Colin Hart, Evelyn Hart, Tim Lippard, Tony Quinn

CONTENTS

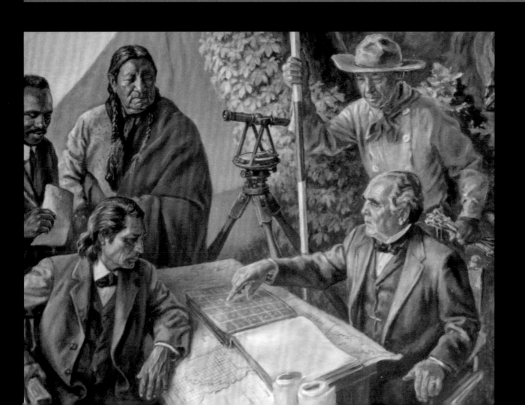

The opening of the Unassigned Lands in 1889 is depicted in this detail from a Charles Banks Wilson mural in the state capitol.
COURTESY OKLAHOMA DEPARTMENT OF TOURISM AND RECREATION; PHOTOGRAPH BY FRED MARVEL.

Building Blocks
of the Past

Hennessey Shale fossil.

Scientists date the sedimentary rocks formed by ancient seas that once covered Oklahoma at more than one billion years old. The up thrusts that formed the state's mountain systems—and corresponding sinking that allowed shallow seas to leave deposits of mud and swamp plants—resulted in expansive deposits of petroleum, shale, limestone, and coal, an important part of the state's modern economy. Fossilized remains of snails, trilobites, and other sea creatures, along with preserved coral reefs, prove the existence of the ancient seas.

A Primitive Amniote

Bones of *Captorhinus* are the most common fossils at Fort Sill. As a result, we can reconstruct entire skeletons using real bone.

The first amniotes, resembling small lizards, evolved from their amphibious ancestors roughly 300 million years ago—in order to adapt to drier environments as the seas receded.

The Wichita Mountains and the Arbuckle Mountains are among the world's oldest mountains, dating from the Pennsylvania Period, 320 million years ago. They were once the size of the Alps until the forces of nature reduced them to exposed outcrops and eroded stumps.

The first humans to arrive in the region were nomadic, following herds of prehistoric animals such as large reptiles and mammoths. Between 20,000 and 2,000 years ago, Folsom hunters, Ozark Bluff Dwellers, and other Archaic people continued their nomadic lifestyle, evidenced by spear points they left from their hunts. About 2,000 years ago, Oklahoma's primitive people abandoned cave and ledge dwellings and began building more permanent structures.

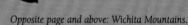

Opposite page and above: Wichita Mountains.

The oldest park in Oklahoma is Turner Falls Park.
The state's largest waterfall is Turner Falls,
just below the Arbuckle Mountains.

Left: The heavily tattooed man clad in feathers and beads was depicted on a shard of pottery found at the site.

Above: Spiro Mounds, located in LeFlore County on the southern bank of the Arkansas River, is considered to be Oklahoma's, most important prehistoric Native American site. The site grew from a small farming village to one of the most important centers in what later became the United States. Between 850 AD and 1450 twelve mounds, ceremonial areas, and a support city were created for the Caddoan-speaking leadership who participated in the Mississippian Culture (also known as the Southeastern Ceremonial Complex, the Southern Death Cult, and the Buzzard Cult). This culture was a loosely organized trading, religious, and political system that included the leadership from many language groups and several million people with trade connections stretching from the Rocky Mountains to the Virginia coast and from the Gulf Coast of Florida to the Great Lakes. Each group was more or less independent although tied to the four regional mound centers. These regional mound centers included Cahokia, where East St. Louis is now, Moundville in Alabama, Etowah in Georgia, and Spiro in eastern Oklahoma. The twelve Spiro Mounds were built in layers from basket loads of dirt. There are three kinds of mounds at the Spiro site: one burial mound, two temple mounds, and nine house mounds. Most of the mounds were for buildings to be placed upon or to cover old houses, but the burial mound attracted the most attention. The site is world renowned for the amazing amount of art and artifacts dug from the burial mound, known as the Craig Mound. Even though Choctaw and Chickasaw freedmen farmed the land within the complex from about the 1870s, the mounds themselves remained undisturbed until 1917. At that time, Joseph Thoburn, who had taken photographs of the site in 1914, tested Ward Mound One, a buried house mound. However, the landowners allowed nothing further until 1933 when a group of commercial diggers called the Pocola Mining Company secured a lease for the Craig Mound. From 1933 until 1935 Pocola employees dug haphazardly into the burial mound, destroying about one-third of the mound. They sold thousands of artifacts, stone, copper, shell, basketry, and fabric, to collectors throughout the world. The site, called "King Tut of the Arkansas Valley" by the Kansas City Star in 1935, was yielding elaborately decorated artifacts in greater numbers and in better states of preservation than any other Mississippian site and the Oklahoma Legislature was finally prevailed upon to pass a licensing requirement for the protection of the site. This resulted in the shutting down of Pocola Mining and halted further destruction of the site. In 1936 the University of Oklahoma (OU) took over scientific excavation of what remained of the burial mound. Until October 1941 OU archaeologists oversaw Works Progress Administration (WPA) workers in investigating the site. From the burial mound more than six hundred complete or partial burials were recovered along with thousands of artifacts. They also worked on the other eight mounds known at the time. The excavations ended in 1941 because of World War II and the end of the WPA. In the mid-1960s there was an aborted effort by the U.S. Army Corps of Engineers to purchase most of the mound center to create a national archaeological park. Finally, in May 1978, the Spiro Mounds Archaeological State Park, with the help of the Oklahoma Archaeological Survey, opened an Interpretive Center as the first and only Oklahoma prehistoric American Indian archaeological site open to the public under the direction of the Oklahoma Tourism and Recreation Department. In 1979 the Oklahoma Archaeological Survey conducted additional research and three more mounds were found. Spiro Mound Group was listed in the National Register of Historic Places in 1969 (NR 69000153). In 1991 administration transferred to the Oklahoma Historical Society with an expanded Interpretive Center and an interpretive trail system allowing visitors to learn about this unique and powerful part of Oklahoma's past. Based on information from the Oklahoma Historical Society.

The Mound Builders constructed huge mounds to serve as homes and religious shrines. They cultivated corn, beans, and squash and developed a complex society. Pottery-making was introduced and bows and arrows replaced spears as the hunting weapon of choice. Woodland people lived in camps and moved when local resources were exhausted.

Ancestors of the Wichita Indians built permanent villages and hunted bison and deer and tended fields of beans, corn, and squash. They built farming villages near rivers and creeks. The area drained by the Canadian and Washita rivers and their tributaries contained many ancient villages.

Right: The Spiro Mounds opened to the public in 1978 and are now under the protection of the Oklahoma Historical Society. Special tours are offered during solstices and equinoxes.

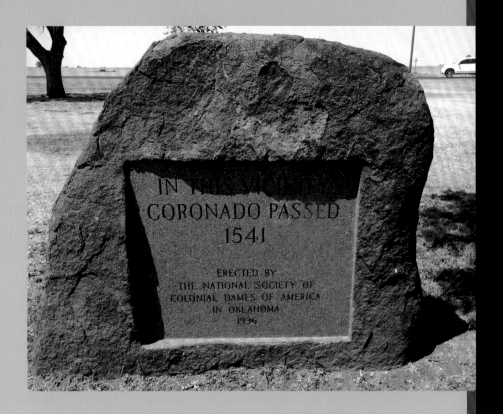

Francisco Vásquez de Coronado was the first European visitor in 1541, crossing the present Oklahoma Panhandle in search of cities of gold. The French replaced the Spanish in exploring Oklahoma in the early 1700s. Bernard de la Harpe visited Indian villages along the Canadian and Arkansas rivers and left behind a journal of immense detail. The French sought to open trade relations with American Indians living in Oklahoma.

Shortly after the United States purchased Louisiana from the French in 1803, President Thomas Jefferson envisioned voluntary removal of American Indians from the southeast part of the nation to satisfy the land hunger of white settlers. Voluntary removal was not successful, so in 1825, with increased pressure to move the Indians westward, Congress set aside a wide swath of land as Indian Territory.

Above: Francisco Vásquez de Coronado was the first European known to have entered what is now Oklahoma, crossing the state in its northwestern corner. He was in search of cities of gold, which of course he did not find. In 1936 the Colonial Dames of America erected a stone monument at a roadside pullover in Beaver County in the Panhandle to mark the passage of Coronado. Later, in the 1700s, the French replaced the Spanish in exploring Oklahoma. Bernard de la Harpe left behind a detailed journal describing the Indian villages he visited. The French were not searching for the cities of gold. They wanted to open trade relations with the American Indians who were then living in the territory that became Oklahoma. It was in 1803 that the United States purchased from the French the area known as the Louisiana Purchase that included Oklahoma.
PHOTOGRAPH COURTESY OF LOU ANN MURPHY.

Right: French traders among the Osage are shown in this detail from Charles Banks Wilson's mural in the state capitol. French coureurs du bois explored the region seeking furs and opening trading posts among the Native Americans. Unlike the Spanish, the French were willing to trade guns and gunpowder to the Indians, touching off a clash between the two European powers for control of the area that was not settled until 1800.
COURTESY OKLAHOMA DEPARTMENT OF TOURISM AND RECREATION; PHOTOGRAPH BY FRED MARVEL.

Left: George Catlin's 1836 painting Cler-Mont, Chief of the Osages. Clermont was a friend of the early American explorers in Oklahoma and welcomed First Lieutenant James B. Wilkinson, the first official American representative to enter Oklahoma, to his village in the fall of 1806. Like most Osage, Clermont's ears had been pierced to support huge earrings that distended his ear lobes with their weight.

COURTESY OF THE GILCREASE MUSEUM.

Below: Traditional Seminole artist Fred Beaver's painting Seminoles Making Sofkey. Sofkey is a traditional Seminole and Creek food staple made by pounding corn into corn meal and then boiling it. After cooling, the meal was dripped through wood ashes and then ground nuts, such as hickory, and bone marrow, were added to form the finished food product. The Seminoles were the last of the Five Tribes to be removed to Oklahoma, with the final band making the journey in 1858. The war fought over their removal was the longest and most costly Indian war in American history. Spread over seven years, the Great Seminole War involved 40,000 American troops and cost between $30 million and $40 million.

COURTESY OF THE GILCREASE MUSEUM.

Above: The Five Civilized Tribes Museum in Muskogee, The five Tribes are the Cherokee, Chickasaw, Choctaw, Muscogee (Creek) and Seminole Tribes.

Below: Trail of Tears by prominent Creek artist Albert Harjo. Clinging to their ancient homeland in Georgia and Alabama the majority of Creeks opposed removal. Following the Creek War of 1836-1840, approximately 14,500 were herded west to their new home in Oklahoma by federal troops during the winter of 1836-1837. No one knows how many died on the Creek Trail of Tears, but 3,500 died of exposure or disease after arriving in their new homeland. The two factions of Creeks were reunited in 1839.

COURTESY OF ALBERT HARJO.

The Five Tribes—the Choctaws, Chickasaws, Creeks, Seminoles, and Cherokees—felt pressure from state and federal government leaders to leave their ancestral home. They negotiated treaties to exchange their lands in the southeastern United States for land in Indian Territory. The Choctaws were the first to accept removal. The forced removal of the Five Tribes was accomplished by military units herding the American Indians westward along the Trail of Tears.

Much sickness and death permeate the sad chapter of history that tells the story of the coming of American Indians to Oklahoma. Many tribal members arrived in their new home with nothing except their horses, mules, wagons, farm implements, and household goods. To accommodate the arrival of the large Five Tribes, American Indian nations such as the Wichita, Osage, and Quapaw were confined by treaty to smaller reservations.

Every first Saturday in May,
the town of Prague, Oklahoma,
celebrates its rich Czech heritage
with a Kolache Festival.

To keep peace in Indian Territory, military roads were constructed and forts were built to house soldiers on the frontier. As roads improved, non-Indian settlers followed the Tribes. They lived in crude shelters and braved the forces of nature to create farms from prairie sod and woodlands.

Opposite: The Fort Reno Chapel.

Above: Formerly the Officers Quarters now the Fort Reno Visitor Center and Museum.

Left: Established in 1824, Fort Gibson remained in service until 1871. During its early history it was the most important military post in Indian Territory. Today it has been restored and operates as the Fort Gibson Military Park.

COURTESY OKLAHOMA DEPARTMENT OF TOURISM AND RECREATION; PHOTOGRAPH BY FRED MARVEL.

Choctaw Statesman Chief Allen Wright.

As railroads were built, more non-Indians, including cattlemen, settled in Oklahoma. Ethnic groups clustered around mineral wealth. The coal fields attracted Italian, Russian, Polish, Irish, and Welsh immigrants. German Mennonites from Russia created their own communities such as Corn, Colony, and Bessie. Czechs founded Yukon and Prague. Several all-black towns were founded by freedmen of the Five Tribes or later arrivals looking for economic opportunities. Even the name Oklahoma comes from American Indian influence on the region, from the Choctaw phrase *okla humma*, literally meaning red people. Choctaw Chief Allen Wright suggested the name in 1866 during treaty negotiations with the federal government.

The heart of central Oklahoma was opened for general settlement by the unique Oklahoma Land Run of 1889. Tens of thousands of home seekers lined up at the four boundaries of the land. Historian Angie Debo wrote, "Men still like to tell how they drove a stake in the prairie, feverishly located cornerstones, and rode to the land office to record their choices. By nightfall, town sites were laid out, lots staked, and tents were set up."

When the sun set, the solitude that had marked these parcels of land for eons was broken by the cheerful confusion of towns that grew by the hour and the campfires of homesteaders. Within days, banks, newspapers, stores, restaurants, and law and doctor offices opened. For a year, the surging frontier had no organized government until Congress, in 1890, organized the Territory of Oklahoma, and added the Panhandle to the new territory.

The people began clamoring for statehood. At first, it was thought that Indian Territory might become the State of Sequoyah and Oklahoma Territory might be the State of Oklahoma. Leaders of the Five Tribes supported the formation of two states. But, because of political reasons, President Theodore Roosevelt insisted that the two territories be combined into one state.

The railroads led the movement for the opening of the Unassigned Lands for homesteaders in the post-Civil War era. By pressuring the federal government to open that part of Oklahoma not occupied by Indian Tribes, the railroad hoped to expand their business in the area. The railroads employed such lobbyists as E. C. Boudinot, a Cherokee, and helped fund such Boomers as David L. Payne to pressure congress to open what became known as "The Promised Land." The actual opening of the Unassigned Lands in 1889 is depicted in this detail from a Charles Banks Wilson mural in the state capitol.

COURTESY OKLAHOMA DEPARTMENT OF TOURISM AND RECREATION, PHOTOGRAPH BY FRED MARVEL.

Frederic Remington's The Stampede. *Cowboying was not the glamorous profession depicted in the movies. The hours were long and hard, and the work was dangerous. A hard fall, especially during a stampede, or "stompedes" as the cowboys called them, usually resulted in serious injury or death. Many stampedes were caused by the spring storms that periodically swept over the plains; however, according to old-time drovers, lightning killed more cowboys. During electrical storms many cowboys would throw away their knives, spurs, or anything else made of metal in the belief that the items attracted lightning. Others put beeswax inside their hats in the belief that the beeswax would not conduct electricity.*

COURTESY OF THE GILCREASE MUSEUM.

William H. "Alfalfa Bill" Murray, Oklahoma's most colorful political leader, chaired the Constitutional Convention that produced a populist state constitution that was the longest in the nation. The people of Oklahoma and Indian territories approved the constitution and elected Oklahoma's first statewide officials. Charles Haskell was elected the first governor and Kate Barnard was elected Commissioner of Charities and Corrections. She was the first woman elected to statewide office in the nation.

A mock wedding between an American Indian maiden and a gentleman symbolized the combining of the two territories. The dream of statehood became a reality on November 16, 1907, when Oklahoma became the forty-sixth state of the Union.

The Camp Cook's Troubles by Charles M. Russell. The horses in the remuda were supposed to be broken and trained, but this was not always the case. In this scene a frightened horse disrupts the morning meal of coffee and eggs. Although Russell portrays the cowboys on the left carrying revolvers, such was not generally the case. Few cowboys owned pistols. They simply could not afford them on their wages of $25 to $40 per month. Those who did usually left them in the chuck wagon. They were too easily lost, and an accidental shot could start a stampede or wound a cowboy, and medical aid was non-existent on most drives. In the event of a serious injury, the trail boss would send for a doctor from the nearest settlement while the cook did what he could. When one cowboy was killed after falling from a horse in the Cherokee Outlet, his foreman had five other cowboys dig the grave. Afterward, the foreman asked "Does anybody know the right words to say?" When no one answered, the foreman continued, "Well, throw some dirt on the son of a gun, and let's get back to work."

A Style
All Its Own

CHAPTER 2

Many events in Oklahoma's history make it unique among the states. From the Trails of Tears that brought American Indians from the southeastern United States to the land runs that opened large areas of the region to non-Indian settlement, the way in which Oklahoma became populated with a diverse citizenry can never be duplicated.

Below: Wetlands—swampy marshes.

Above: The world's tallest hill is Cavanal Hill in Poteau. At 1,999 feet, it is one foot less than the official definition of a mountain.

Right: Purple coneflower.

Right: Indian Paintbrush.

Even the shape of Oklahoma is unique. When the Panhandle was added to Oklahoma Territory in 1890, the shape of the future state was forever forged. Cimarron County in the Panhandle is the only county in the United States that touches four other states, New Mexico, Texas, Colorado, and Kansas.

Oklahoma is the twentieth largest state with 69,898 square miles. The variety of vegetation, topsoil, and climate is like no other state. Oklahoma has twelve distinct ecosystems, from the arid, flat land of the Panhandle to the swampy marshes of McCurtain County. The Ouachita and Ozark mountains are the only major mountainous region between the Rocky Mountains and Appalachians. The world's tallest hill is Cavanal Hill (above) in Poteau. At 1,999 feet, it is one foot less than the official definition of a mountain.

Kiamichi Country

Opposite page and this page: Kiamichi is a former community in northern Pushmataha County, Oklahoma, six miles east of Tuskahoma. Kiamichi Country was so named because of the Kiamichi Mountains, but as of 2015 the official designation is Choctaw Country.

Forests cover one fourth of the state. There is sparse rainfall in the western counties, but some places in eastern Oklahoma average more than fifty inches of rainfall annually, supporting a wide range of trees, flowers, grasslands, and wildlife.

Opposite: Hardwood reforestation in southeastern Oklahoma.

This page, clockwise, starting from the top:

The ATV trails at Little Sahara State Park in northwestern Oklahoma.

Sandstone in central Oklahoma.

Residents of some of the nation's largest prairie dog towns near the Wichita Mountains.

In southeastern Oklahoma logging and sawmills and paper plants have been thriving for over a century. Many of the huge trees are gone, but where trees are removed reforestation is ongoing.

Lake Murray

Arkansas River

Below: Red Bud Tree at Cedar Lake in Ouachita National Forest.

Southeast Riverway

Above and below: Ouachita National Forest

Above and below: Talimena National Scenic Byway

Oklahoma City Skyline

Oklahoma has 598 incorporated towns. Two of the nation's top fifty cities in population, Oklahoma City and Tulsa, are located within the state. Oklahoma City is the largest city. Fifty-eight percent of Oklahomans live within the metropolitan areas of Oklahoma City and Tulsa.

Tulsa
Hard Rock Hotel

Tulsa Riverwalk

Oklahoma's people are unique. The state has the second-highest number of American Indians. With a population estimated in 2013 at 3,823,819, Oklahoma ancestral makeup was above ten percent for each of German, American, Irish, English, African American, and American Indian groups. The state's first century has made Oklahomans creative, resilient, hard-working, strong in spirit, and just plain tough.

SYLVAN NATHAN GOLDMAN

Sylvan N. Goldman was born in Ardmore, Chickasaw Nation, prior to statehood, to parents Michael and Hortense Goldman. He attended Ardmore schools and as a youth worked in the dry goods store owned by his father and uncle.

He served in France during World War I and after the war he and his older brother opened a wholesale fruits and produce business in Texas. The brothers moved to California and were there introduced to a new type of grocery store offering all products under one roof, the supermarket. They returned to Oklahoma bringing this new concept of shopping to their home state. They opened their first store in Tulsa in 1920 under the corporate name of Sun Grocery Company. In only one year there were twenty more Sun Groceries throughout the state. The brothers later sold their company to Skaggs-Safeway stores and in 1934 Sylvan bought and revived the floundering Humpty Dumpty chain.

In 1936 he came up with his most important contribution to grocery shopping, the grocery cart, now used worldwide. One of his original carts can be seen at the Greater Southwest Historical Museum in Ardmore, his hometown. Through the Folding Basket Carrier Company that he created in order to manufacture the carts, there ensued many other items that revolutionized grocery shopping.

He and his wife were avid patrons of the arts and throughout his lifetime he received many honors for his innovative and philanthropic contributions, including being inducted into Oklahoma Hall of Fame in 1971. Perhaps one of his most important contributions was $1.5 million dollars to the Sylvan N. Goldman Center to house the Oklahoma Blood Institute, the ninth largest blood donation center in the country and an institute pivotal to saving lives on a daily basis.

CARLTON COLE MAGEE

Carlton Cole Magee invented the first parking meter in 1932 in response to the growing problem of parking congestion. He patented it in 1935. As head of the city's chamber of commerce, Magee hoped the meters would free up parking spaces for local businesses. Holger George Thuesen and Gerald A. Hale designed the first working meter, the Black Maria. Thuesen and Hale were engineering professors at Oklahoma A & M and began working on the parking meter in 1933 at the request of Carl C. Magee. They.started the Magee-Hale Park-O-Meter Company to manufacture the parking meters. These early parking meters were produced at factories in Oklahoma City and Tulsa, Oklahoma. The first was installed on July 16, 1935 in Magee's hometown, Oklahoma City at First Street and Robinson Avenue. It is estimated today that there are more than five million meters in use in the United States.

Inventions & Innovation

WILEY POST

Wiley Post was born in Texas, but Oklahomans claimed him as their own, often referring to him as the world's greatest pilot. And who is to argue? After all, he was the first man to fly alone around the earth. Additionally, he was a parachute jumper, a test pilot, the discoverer of the jet stream, and the inventor of the pressurized flight suit. And he accomplished all that in thirty-six years. He was killed in a plane crash in Point Barrow, Alaska, with another famed Oklahoman, Will Rogers, on August 15, 1935.

CLARENCE NASH

Clarence Charles "Ducky" Nash, whose nickname derived from the fact that he is best known as the voice of Donald Duck, was born in 1904 in Watonga, Oklahoma (now the state's cheese capital). A street in that town is named for him. "Ducky" provided the voice of Donald for fifty years, as well as being the original voice of Tom in *Tom and Jerry* cartoons. Known principally as a voice actor, he provided the voices for many other characters during a career that ended with his death in 1985.

GARY ENGLAND

A native of Seiling, Oklahoma and University of Oklahoma graduate, Gary England has been protecting the people of Oklahoma through his weather broadcasts since joining the Channel 9 TV news team as director of meteorology in 1972. He has a very long list of credits to his name in the field of weather, including being the first to use Doppler Radar to alert viewers of impending tornadoes. He was selected for induction into the Oklahoma Hall of Fame in November of 2013. In 2013 he also retired as chief meteorologist for Channel 9 and assumed new duties with Griffin Communications, Channel 9's parent company.

He joins a long list of Oklahomans recognized by the Oklahoma Hall of Fame which has honored more than 670 Oklahomans since its founding in 1927, names like noted author Ralph Ellison, radio announcer Paul Harvey, and Cincinnati Reds' catcher Johnny Bench. Hall of Fame inductees' names are on display at the Gaylord-Pickens Museum, along with busts and portraits. Granite monuments also honor these individuals in the Heritage Plaza at the Oklahoma State Fairgrounds.

Oklahomans always have been forward-thinking. They have dared to dream beyond confining lines drawn by custom and tradition. Most students of Oklahoma's colorful past know about some unique inventions such as the shopping cart, the twisty tie, the parking meter, and Wiley Post's pioneering first solo flight around the world and the discovery of the jet stream. But there are so many more innovations.

America's first shelterbelt was built in Oklahoma during the Great Depression to stop the wind from blowing topsoil from the land. L. A. Macklanbug invented and patented weather stripping after his wife grew frustrated because the Oklahoma wind constantly blew dust around the front door into their new home.

When floodwaters swept away crops and land, Oklahoma became the site of the first upstream dam-flood protection projects. When tornadoes threatened Oklahomans' lives, meteorologist Gary England developed common visual warning signs for television, now in use worldwide.

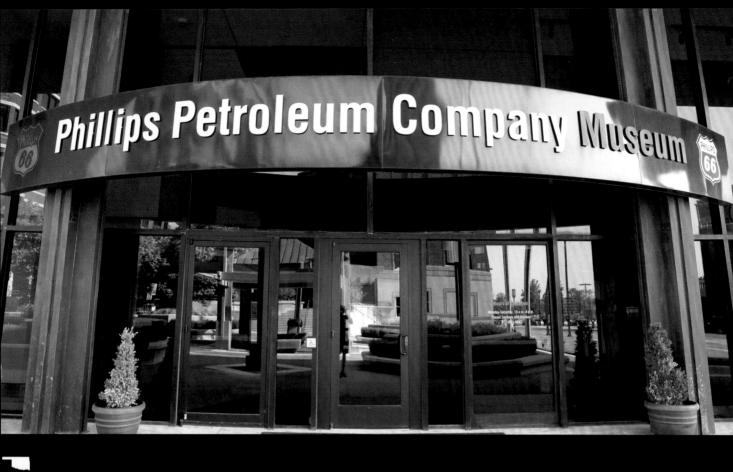

Above: The Phillips Petroleum Company Museum.

Below: The Frank Phillips Home in Bartlesville. Frank Phillips started his career as a barber in Iowa. He came to Bartlesville in 1903 hoping to discover oil. None of the wells he financed were successful until more than two years later. Then he hit pay dirt, finding oil in the next eighty-one wells he drilled. This was the foundation for his wealth and the Phillips Petroleum Company which was founded in 1917 and put Bartlesville on the map.

Inventions & Innovation

The needs and wants of consumers spawned ideas in Oklahoma. Scientists at Phillips Petroleum in Bartlesville invented the aerosol can and plastic. The idea for mud flaps to prevent the wheels of big rigs from kicking up mud and rocks came from Oscar March, a truck driver at Tinker Air Force Base in Midwest City. Perry machine shop owner Ed Malzahn created the Ditch Witch trenching machine to replace the pick and shovel. Now half the trenching machines in the world are made at the Ditch Witch plant in Perry.

The shopping cart and the parking meter were invented in Oklahoma City.

In 1932, Walt Disney chose Clarence Nash, a native of Watonga, as the voice of Donald Duck. For the next fifty years, Nash was the voice of the famous cartoon duck.

NEXRAD (next generation weather radar) was invented by professors at the University of Oklahoma School of Meteorology. The National Weather Service Forecast Center is on the OU campus in Norman.

Clinton Riggs designed the YIELD sign and first used it in Tulsa.

The world's first tornado forecast was issued by two officers at Tinker Air Force Base in Midwest City in 1948.

Arthur Jones, a native of Seminole, invented Nautilus exercise equipment found in most gyms and health spas in the nation.

The first Sam's Club warehouse shopping store was built in Midwest City in 1983 and opened by founder, Kingfisher native Sam Walton.

Oklahoma's State Capitol is the only such building located over a commercial pool of oil.

America's first Boy Scout troop was formed at Pawhuska.

The first Girl Scout cookie was sold in Muskogee in 1917.

Above: The National Weather Service Forecast Center is in Norman.

SAMUEL MOORE WALTON

Kingfisher, Oklahoma is proud to claim Sam Walton as a native son. He was born there in 1918 to Thomas Gibson and Nancy Lee Walton, Even though the family moved when Sam was a boy he never forgot his Kingfisher roots and was a frequent visitor there throughout his life.

With extensive retail experience behind him, Sam Walton and a brother opened the first Walmart in Rogers, Arkansas, calling it Walmart Discount City. From that humble beginning, the worldwide chain now known simply as Walmart was born. One might wonder what Sam Walton would think of his stores today since his determination to market American-made products and find American manufacturers, has definitely been forgotten.

Sam's Clubs, membership only retail warehouse stores, operated by Walmart and named for Sam, was founded in 1983, nine years before his death, and as of 2014 had grown to over 600 stores in forty-eight states, 11 in Puerto Rico, 13 in Brazil, and 1 in China.

No other state has had a greater impact on America's space program than Oklahoma. Even before rockets sent astronauts hurtling toward outer space, Oklahoma's pioneer aviators Tom and Paul Braniff were building Braniff Airways and Wiley Post was discovering the jet stream and developing the pressurized flying suit. In 1933, Post made the first solo airplane flight around the world, an unimaginable feat at the time.

Oklahoma has had more astronauts than any other state. Leroy Gordon Cooper was chosen in the first group of seven American astronauts. Jerrie Cobb was among the elite of women pilots and was the first woman to pass NASA astronaut training tests. Colonel Jack Ridley was the test pilot and project engineer who made it possible for the sound barrier to be broken in 1947.

Shannon Lucid holds the record for most time in space for a female astronaut. Thomas Stafford paved the way for the lunar landing with his command of *Apollo 10*. John Herrington was the first American Indian astronaut and Donna Shirley was project manager for the innovative exploration of the planet Mars with a robotic rover.

Top: The General Thomas P. Stafford Air and Space Museum located in Weatherford, Oklahoma.

Above: Aviator Geraldyn "Jerrie" Cobb was born in Norman, Oklahoma.
PHOTOGRAPH COURTESY OF MUSEUM OF WOMEN PILOTS.

Right: Astronaut Leroy Gordon Cooper, Jr., was born in Shawnee, Oklahoma.

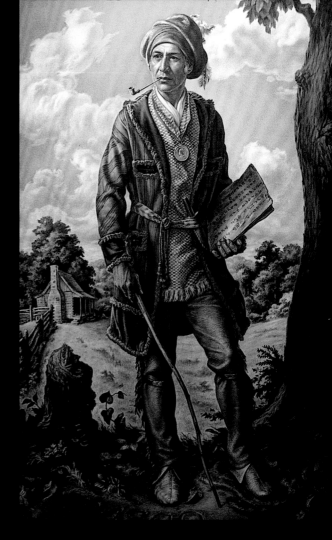

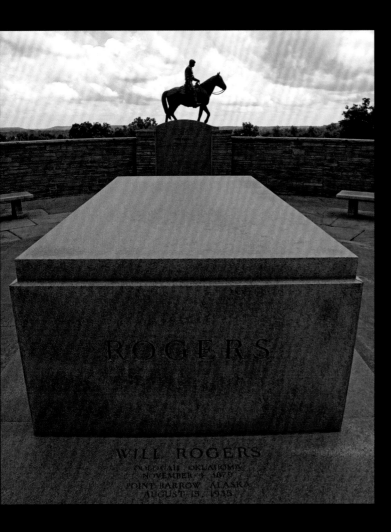

Will Rogers is generally acknowledged as Oklahoma's favorite son. A veteran of vaudeville, he starred in seventy-one movies, was the highest paid movie star of his day, wrote more than 4,000 newspaper columns, and was beloved by most Americans. When he and fellow Oklahoman Wiley Post were killed in an airplane crash in Alaska in 1935, Rogers' daily column was read by one-third of the nation's population. His statue, along with a statue of Cherokee educator Sequoyah, appears in Statuary Hall in the United States Capitol.

Oklahomans have changed the direction of American music. Woody Guthrie, Charlie Christian, and Bob Wills created new styles of music. Today, country music is dominated by Oklahoma artists such as Carrie Underwood, Garth Brooks, Vince Gill, Reba McEntire, Blake Shelton, and Toby Keith.

Fueling a Dynamic Economy

Tinker Air Force Base.

CHAPTER

3

Primarily an agricultural state through the first half of the twentieth century, Oklahoma has assumed a broader economic structure since 1950. Oklahoma government and private sector leaders have identified five major wealth-creating parts of the state economy: aerospace and defense, energy, agriculture and biosciences, information and financial services, and transportation and distribution.

Even though no state's economy is recession-proof, Oklahoma has come close with diversity, by creating a young and growing work force of educated professionals with skills that transfer to other industries when downturns occur in a particular industry. The state has six military bases that serve as a major driver of economic development. The largest is Tinker Air Force Base in Midwest City.

Unemployment levels have trended about three percentage points below the national average for the past several years. Underlying much of the optimism about the state's economic future is the belief that the old days of boom and bust in the oil and gas industry are gone. Any boom experienced in the all important energy sector will be tempered from time to time by normal business cycles, but the severe downturns that plagued the state several times during its first century are not coming back.

Energy officials believe that new drilling technologies will prevent busts by maintaining steady production. Previous price spikes were caused by shortages, which now can be avoided. New methods of seismic underground mapping, horizontal drilling, and more-precise hydraulic fracturing are tools that will increase production and drive down prices.

Oklahoma has been a major player in oil and gas production for its life as a state. More than a dozen of the largest natural gas fields ever discovered in the nation are within the boundaries of Oklahoma. The petroleum-rich history of the state produced leaders who made fortunes from pulling crude and gas from beneath the surface. John W. Nichols, a young accountant in Oklahoma City, and co-founder of Devon Energy, won approval by the Securities and Exchange Commission of the first oil and gas funding proposal. The idea changed the way that oil and gas production was financed around the world.

The names of oil and gas pioneers in Oklahoma read like a "Who's Who" in oil and gas history. J. Paul Getty and T. Boone Pickens became two of the world's richest men. Harry Sinclair founded the Sinclair Oil Company. The company that became Conoco was born in the Osage County oilfields drilled by E. W. Marland. Robert S. Kerr and Dean A. McGee created Kerr-McGee Corporation. Frank and L. E. Phillips formed Phillips Petroleum Company. Devon Energy, Chesapeake Energy, SandRidge Energy, and the Williams Companies, some of Oklahoma's most powerful companies, are among the elite of America's petroleum giants.

Opposite page top: Devon Energy Center, a fifty-story skyscraper in Oklahoma City.

Opposite page, bottom left and right: Devon Energy Center interior during the Christmas holidays.

Above: Oklahoma's oil and gas industry is evident all over the state.

The strength and diversity of Oklahoma's energy is delivered in many forms—natural gas, oil, wind, and electricity.

Right: The Clean Energy® fueling station at Oklahoma State University allows drivers to fill their vehicles with compressed natural gas or CNG.

Below and bottom: The huge presence of natural gas processing facilities that dot the Oklahoma countryside.

Opposite: Electric grids crisscross Oklahoma.

At one time during the early oil and gas booms, the state provided as much as ten percent of the nation's petroleum production. Currently, the state ranks fourth in the nation for production of natural gas and fifth in the production of crude oil. The largest Oklahoma-based companies are energy related.

Eight percent of America's natural gas liquid reserves are located in the state. Oklahoma is leading a coalition of twenty-two states to combine purchasing power to drive down the price of automobiles and trucks powered by compressed natural gas (CNG). A Honda Civic powered by CNG was driven 228 miles for $5.32. It was one of the models added to the state automobile fleet. In her State of the State message in 2013, Oklahoma Governor Mary Fallin announced the delivery of hundreds of CNG-powered state vehicles and speculated about the tremendous savings to state taxpayers if eventually all such vehicles were powered by natural gas produced from beneath the surface of Oklahoma.

There is no doubt about the importance of the oil and gas industry to Oklahoma's economy. One in six jobs in the state is directly or indirectly supported by oil and gas. Since 2009, oil and gas companies have added nearly 12,000 jobs, the average oil and gas worker makes more than $113,000 per year, and annual operations from the oil and natural gas industry generate $52 billion in goods and services—one third of the state's gross state product. In addition, Oklahoma oil and gas producers pay nearly $1 billion in gross production taxes each year.

From early day
windmills to today's wind
farms that dot the western
plains, the people of Oklahoma
have been harnessing the
wind that comes roaring
down the plains.

Top: Grain silos.

Above: Tuttle Grain & Supply located in Tuttle, Oklahoma.

Agriculture remains an integral part of the Oklahoma economy. The state's top five agricultural products are cattle and calves, swine, broiler chickens, wheat, and dairy products. State beef cattle producers are fifth in the nation in supplying beef for America's tables. The state is eighth in swine production.

Racing and grazing…

Slew City Sir is a grandson of Seattle Slew, the only undefeated Triple Crown winner.

Oklahoma's most valuable crop is wheat and the state ranks fourth in the nation in wheat production. Greenhouse and nursery products are an important part of the agricultural economy with hay, cotton, soybeans, corn, pecans, grain sorghum, peanuts, peaches, oats, and watermelons as major crops. The state has 83,000 farms, collectively adding more than $6 billion to the state's gross domestic product.

Oklahoma grown can be found in farmer's markets and produce stands throughout the state—from spring through fall.

Above: Tree farm.

Left: The vinyard of the Canadian River Winery in Slaughterville. This winery is Oklahoma's second oldest.

Opposite, top: Mister Lew *is a towing vessel.*

Opposite, bottom: International Paper, Valliant, Oklahoma.

Below: US Silica, Mill Creek, Oklahoma.

Manufacturing adds many jobs in the state. Production of machinery, particularly oil field machinery, has grown in recent decades. Construction machinery, machine parts, and refrigeration and heating equipment are other types of machinery manufactured in the state. After oil field machinery, aircraft and aerospace equipment manufacturing ranks second. Other manufactured items include computer and electronic equipment, fabricated metal products, processed foods, and rubber and plastic products. The state is the top manufacturer of tires in North America.

Foreign investment in Oklahoma has been an economic shot in the arm over the past few years. The state is home to more than 140 U.S. subsidiaries of foreign companies. The investment of global companies has added nearly 37,000 jobs in the past half dozen years.

In 2011, Oklahoma exported more than $6.2 billion in products and services. Nearly one-fourth of manufacturing workers in the state depended upon exports for their jobs. More than 2,000 companies exported goods from Oklahoma. Of those, eighty-five percent were small and medium-sized companies.

Michelin Tire Plant
Ardmore, Oklahoma

Robert S. Kerr Dam

Above: Cherokee Casino, Ramona, Oklahoma.

Left: Major league horseracing at Remington Park: Racing & Casino.

Oklahoma has a civilian labor force of approximately 1.7 million. The government sector provides the most jobs, followed by transportation and utilities, and education, business, and manufacturing. The growing aerospace industry generates more than $11 billion annually. Tulsa is home to the largest airline maintenance base in the world, the global maintenance and engineering headquarters for American Airlines. Aerospace accounts for more than ten percent of the state's industrial output, placing Oklahoma in the top ten nationally in aerospace engine manufacturing.

Oklahoma City Riverwalk

Expo Square, Tulsa

Creating the Atmosphere for Growth

CHAPTER 4

In the second decade of the new century, Oklahoma has one of the strongest economies in the nation. That lofty position did not come by accident—it is the result of a focused and strategic plan. The private sector has linked arms with state government to create a friendly environment for new and expanding business. The Pew Center said Oklahoma was "the best place in the world to do business in oil and gas."

There are many factors that make the atmosphere for growth in Oklahoma so promising. In 2012, *Forbes* Magazine ranked the state third among all the states in the category of overall economic climate for business. The Kauffman Foundation labeled Oklahoma "the friendliest state toward small business."

Opposite: Welding on oil tank.

Below: Choctaw construction.

Also in 2012, Oklahoma was fourth in the nation in creating new jobs and was consistently ranked by national surveys as one of the top ten states for doing business of all kinds. Quality of life, low taxes, low cost of plentiful labor, and almost unlimited sources of power and other utilities were cited as some of the reasons for the state's favorable business climate. A strong statewide chamber of commerce organization has brought businesses of all sizes together to work for one common goal—create more quality jobs.

Below: Newcastle Power Plant.

The electric grids that cross the state are an example of the energy presence throughout Oklahoma.

Oklahoma's cost of living is a major factor in attracting employers to look at Oklahoma for new investment. Oklahomans pay $1,039 less per person in state and local taxes than the nation. Per capita property taxes in the state are the third lowest in the United States and the corporate tax burden is the tenth lowest in the nation.

In 2013 business journals ranked Oklahoma's capital city, Oklahoma City, No. 1 in its economic ranking of the top 102 American cities with population of more than 500,000. Oklahoma City was just one of four large American cities with an unemployment rate of 4.5 percent or lower. The city placed fourth in increase in private sector jobs and led the nation in growth of retail employment. In the ranking, Oklahoma City scored better than Austin, Dallas, and Houston, Texas; Pittsburgh, Pennsylvania; Boston, Massachusetts; and Nashville, Tennessee. A sign of the strength

of the Oklahoma economy was Tulsa's No. 5 ranking in the same national survey. Oklahoma and Texas were the only states that had two cities ranked in the Top Ten best economies.

Oklahoma state government has developed focused plans for providing incentive programs to attract new and expanding business. The incentives range from cash to tax credits. Qualifying businesses can often take advantage of both. Leaders recognize that the creation of jobs triggers other investment and a healthy economy.

Oklahoma workers always have been known for an extraordinary level of proficiency, productivity, and reliability. They contribute their experience, skills, and dedication to the success of a wide variety of technologically advanced industries. The skills come at a competitive wage rate because of Oklahoma's cost of living which is significantly lower than comparable states.

Opposite, top: Sand mining.

Opposite, bottom: Wynnewood Refinery.

Above: Western Farmers Electric Cooperative, coal.

Above: Port of Catoosa.

Below: Muskogee Port.

Education has been a key tool in preparing the state's workforce for cutting edge business growth. Oklahoma's system of 25 public colleges and universities and 57 career and technology centers, and several high-quality private universities, educates students of all ages in the areas needed for today's information-based technology-driven companies.

Southwestern Oklahoma State University in Weatherford.

Southwestern Oklahoma State University

Tulsa Community College

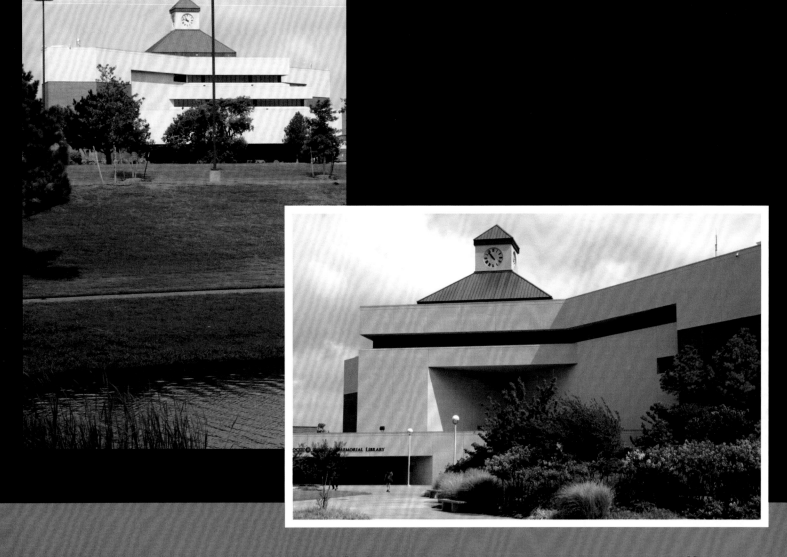

Oklahoma City Community College

University of Tulsa

Langston University

Oklahoma State University

University of Oklahoma

Oklahoma's location makes the state an easily accessible profit center with connections to more than eighty million people within a 500-mile radius. Equidistant between New York City, Los Angeles, Mexico City, and Canada, the state is in a perfect position to serve the nation, North America, and the world. Oklahoma is well suited to deliver and receive goods from around the globe through a comprehensive network of air, ground, water, and rail transportation systems. The McClellan-Kerr Arkansas River Navigation System links ports in northeast Oklahoma with New Orleans and the entire world.

Inside the state, the Oklahoma Department of Transportation has embarked upon an eight-year plan to improve the infrastructure, including an aggressive initiative to repair all structurally deficient highway bridges.

International airports in Oklahoma City and Tulsa and 149 public-use airports around the state provide worldwide access. Twenty rail operators provide Class I and II service throughout the state.

The business friendly atmosphere of the state has been enhanced by an Oklahoma Department of Commerce program called "LocateOK." The agency highlights project-ready certified sites that are immediately available for sale or lease, ready to build on with all utilities in place, or pre-permitted or planned. Even state regulatory hurdles have been cleared for a prospective employer that wants to launch its business without years of delay. LocateOK is far better than the old method of just providing new and expanding businesses with a list of available properties.

Opposite page: Will Rogers World Airport, Oklahoma City.

Below: Tulsa Air and Space Museum.

Downtown Tulsa

Oklahoma electric rates are among the nation's lowest and a modern delivery system allows any size business to be added with almost unlimited energy resources available. State and local governments have emphasized industrial development by making available more than 300 industrial parks and hundreds of office, plant, and building sites ready for business at locations statewide. In addition, Oklahoma is a right-to-work state where workers are allowed to seek or retain employment regardless of union membership requirements.

The efforts of business and government leaders are paying off as new investment decisions are announced. In the first quarter of 2013, thirty company locations announced growth in the state totaling more than $417 million. Six of the locations were new to the state and sixteen were manufacturing companies. It was estimated that the one quarter's new investment would result in more than 3,000 new jobs. The largest job announcements were Paycom in Oklahoma City, Verizon in Tulsa, and ABB in Bartlesville.

The ABB announcement of nearly 300 jobs is an example of Oklahoma attracting international development. ABB is a century-old company based in Switzerland that is a leader in power and automation technology.

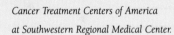

Cancer Treatment Centers of America at Southwestern Regional Medical Center.

Right: Oklahomans are determined to make Oklahoma a fine place to live and raise their families.

Tulsa Rose Garden

BOK Center, Tulsa

General Electric recently announced the establishment of a Global Research Center in the Oklahoma City area to focus on the oil and gas sector to spur economic growth and continue to enhance Oklahoma's reputation as a global hub for energy companies.

Projections from the Oklahoma Department of Commerce predict a bright economic future for the state as Oklahoma's population is projected to top five million by the time the state celebrates its 150th birthday in 2057.

By the 2020 Census, Oklahoma's population will top 4 million.

By the mid 2050s, Oklahoma's population will top 5 million.

By 2075, Oklahoma's population will top 5.5 million.

Oklahoma's population is forecast to grow at an average annual rate of 0.73 percent over the next sixty-five years. With a quality of life second to none and a pro-business atmosphere, the sky is the limit for Oklahoma

Diverse Communities and Fascinating Places

Beavers Bend
State Park

The quality of life in Oklahoma is unsurpassed. Residents and visitors have an unlimited choice of places to visit and celebrations to attend. Reasonable costs, the lack of traffic jams, and plenty of wide, open spaces make outdoor or indoor venues perfect for sightseeing, recreation, or entertainment. Oklahoma has more man-made lakes than any state in the nation and a festival almost every weekend. Visitors may indulge in local specialties at tasteful events such as the Rush Springs Watermelon Festival, Watonga Cheese Festival, or El Reno's Onion-Fried Burger Days.

This page: Beavers Bend State Park near Broken Bow Lake in southeastern Oklahoma.

Lake Tenkiller State Park in Eastern Oklahoma.

Robbers Cave State Park

Boiling Springs State Park

Above: Boiling Springs State Park, Woodward, northwestern Oklahoma.

Lake Wister State Park

Above: Lincoln Bridge, Chickasaw National Recreation Area, Sulphur, Oklahoma.

Left: The Lincoln Bridge was featured on a 2011 National Parks series quarter.

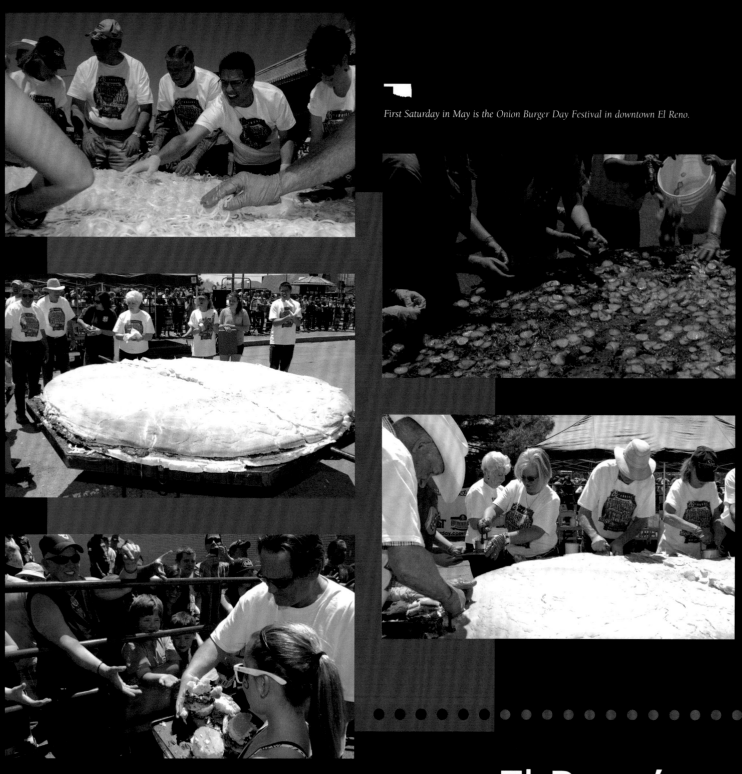

First Saturday in May is the Onion Burger Day Festival in downtown El Reno.

El Reno's
Onion Burger Day

Renaissance
Festival

Above: Balloon fest in Poteau.

Bottom, left: Traveling aerial stunt performers at the balloon fest in Poteau.

Bottom, right: A unicyclist street performer in Oklahoma City.

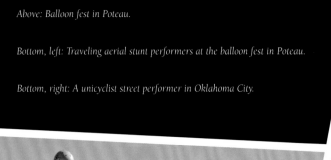

Top: Oklahoma State Fair.

Above: Oklahomans and visitors to the state annually gather at the Gaylord-Pickens Museum, home of the Oklahoma Hall of Fame, for the Statehood Day Festival and Young Entrepreneurs and Artists Market.

Opposite and above: Festival of the Arts, Oklahoma City

Frontier Country

Oklahoma has divided its six regions into "countries." Each has a distinct heritage and flavor and celebrates its heritage in diverse ways. Thirty five state parks, six national protected regions, two national protected forests or grasslands, and a network of wildlife preserves and conservation areas give Oklahoma an unimaginable variety of places to roam. Six percent of the forest land in the state is public land, including the western portions of the Ouachita National Forest, the largest and oldest national forest in the South.

Central Oklahoma, called Frontier Country, is home to the state capital, Oklahoma City, and is a melting pot of people and cultures. The region's history in unique—much of it was opened by the Oklahoma Land Run of 1889. As many as 75,000 people made the historic run on horseback, foot, and mule, and by wagon, buggy, and bicycle. By nightfall, 50,000 settlers called Oklahoma their home.

The region has come a long way since the Land Run, but the enterprising spirit and multicultural riches of the people continue. Oklahoma's largest population groups include people of English, Irish, German, and American Indian descent.

Above: Interior of the state capitol building.

Below: Exterior of the state capitol building.

Above: Canal in downtown Oklahoma City in the daytime.

Below: Canal in downtown Oklahoma City in the nighttime.

Above: The First State Capital Building in Guthrie.

Below: Chesapeake Arena, home of the Oklahoma City Thunder.

The state's first capital, Guthrie, has more buildings on the National Register of Historic Places that any city its size in America. A $1 billion renewal of Oklahoma City's downtown has resulted in a world-class arena for its NBA basketball team and a thriving Bricktown area with restaurants, shopping, canal boat rides, and nightlife.

Downtown Guthrie

Top, right: Masonic Temple in Guthrie.

Oklahoma City National Memorial and Museum

One of the most poignant and powerful places to visit in Oklahoma City is the Oklahoma City National Memorial and Museum, a lasting tribute to the 168 men, women, and children killed in the bombing of the Alfred P. Murrah Federal Building in Oklahoma City on April 19, 1995.

Green Country

The charming towns and sophisticated cities in northeast Oklahoma, Green Country, are a direct result of the excitement of the early part of the twentieth century when the area became one of the richest oil and gas producing regions in North America. Tulsa became "The Oil Capital of the World" and the wealth that followed helped create fabulous museums such as Philbrook and Gilcrease. The OK Mozart International Festival is held each year in Bartlesville and is a jewel among a crown of artistic performances in the region.

Green Country is home to three major American Indian nations—the Cherokee, the Muscogee (Creek), and the Osage—who make up more than ten percent of the region's population. The nations have preserved their heritage with festivals and museums. The region also is home to nearly half of Oklahoma's state parks.

Above: Gilcrease Museum in Tulsa.

Left and below: Phillbrook Museum of Art.

Above: Rafting on the Illinois River.

Right: Downtown Bartlesville.

Below: Cherokee Capital Square in Tahlequah.

Old South. The coal-mining heritage of areas near McAlester produced a diversity of citizens in Choctaw Country. Krebs was settled by Italian immigrants and is famous for its Italian eateries.

Above: There are many species of trees in Beavers Bend State Park.

Left: Durant's Centennial horse.

Opposite: Elk and bison sculptures adorn the grounds of the Choctaw Casino in Durant.

Chickasaw Country

South central Oklahoma, or Chickasaw Country, was the home to the Chickasaws after the federal government moved many Tribes of American Indians to Oklahoma in the nineteenth century. Today, the Chickasaw Nation is a powerful force in the Oklahoma economy. Its WinStar World Casino at Thackerville is the largest casino in the United States and the second-largest in the world. Other casinos such as the Riverwind near Norman draw hundreds of thousands of visitors and provide a first-class entertainment venue.

The region's past is preserved at the Greater Southwest Historical Museum in Ardmore and the Chickasaw Cultural Center in Sulphur. Many lakes and camping areas dot Chickasaw Country. The Arbuckle Mountains, considered to be among the oldest mountains in the world, feature the seventy-seven foot Turner Falls. Farming and ranching are still big business in the area. Garvin and Grady counties are the nation's major suppliers of broomcorn.

This page: WinStar World Casino in Thackerville.

Above: Piominko, *Great Chief of the Chickasaw Nation, by Enoch Kelly Haney is erected at the site of the Chickasaw Nation Capital in Tishomingo, Johnston County, Oklahoma.*

Top right and right: Chickasaw Cultural Center, Sulphur, Oklahoma.

Below: Chickasaw Artesian Hotel, Casino and Spa, Sulphur, Oklahoma.

Great Plains Country

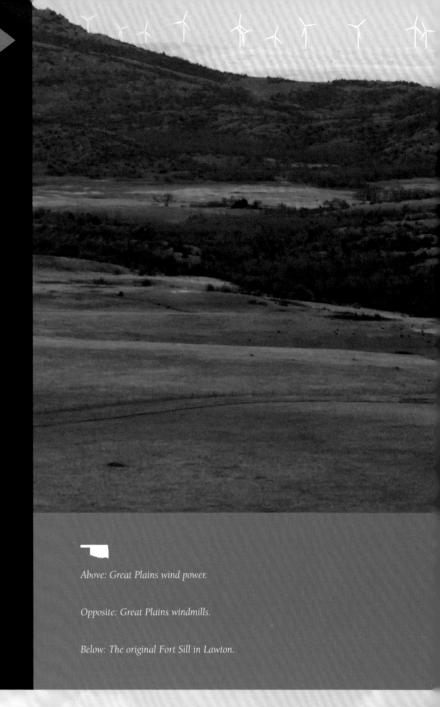

A unique blend of American Indian and cowboy life gave southwest Oklahoma, Great Plains Country, a rich and colorful Western heritage. In the middle of the nineteenth century, few people lived in the region, except for prospectors looking for gold in the Wichita Mountains. Then, the federal government set aside large tracts of land for the Plains Indians—the Comanche, the Kiowa, the Apache, and the Cheyenne.

When white settlers were attracted to the area, a string of forts was built by the U.S. Army to keep the peace. In 1902, Fort Sill at Lawton became the Army's main artillery training center. Today, Fort Sill and Altus Air Force Base are thriving modern military installations.

Above: Great Plains wind power.

Opposite: Great Plains windmills.

Below: The original Fort Sill in Lawton.

Great Plains Country continued

Agriculture continues to be the backbone of the economy in Great Plains Country. With the help of irrigation, cotton, wheat, and hay for cattle make up a major part of the farm production. The Wichita Mountains Wildlife Refuge, where buffalo, longhorn cattle, deer, and elk freely roam, was set aside for federal protection by President Theodore Roosevelt in 1905. The Chisholm Trail Heritage Center in Duncan preserves the exciting story of the Chisholm Trail that ran through Great Plains Country and carried millions of cattle from Texas to railheads in Kansas in the decades after the Civil War.

Right: Buffalo on the Great Plains.

Below: The Chisolm Trail Heritage Center in Duncan.

Opposite, top: Buffalo on the Great Plains.

Opposite, bottom: Longhorn.

Red Carpet Country

The diversity of northwest Oklahoma, Red Carpet Country, ranges from Alabaster Caverns, with the largest gypsum cave in the world, to an unexpected Italianate marble mansion, the Marland Mansion, in Ponca City. The shallow sea that covered the region in the ancient past colored the soil a deep red brown, hence the name "red carpet."

The Panhandle's Black Mesa, the state's highest point, is a lava-topped natural monument created by an ancient volcano. Nearby, dinosaur footprints testify to wildlife visitors of 100 million years ago. Like the land they occupy, the people of northwest Oklahoma are hearty and independent.

Agriculture always has bloomed in Red Carpet Country. Enid, the center of the nation's wheat-producing region, has the third highest amount of elevator space of any city in America. The elevators, the skyscrapers of the Plains, stand as a symbol of the agricultural abundance of this part of Oklahoma.

Higher education is affordable and convenient in Oklahoma. The U.S. Chamber of Commerce ranks the state's system of 25 public colleges and universities No. 7 in affordability and No. 8 in efficiency nationally. Oklahoma's system of career and technology education is often used as a model for other states and foreign countries. The 57 career and technology education campus sites and 16 skills centers in correctional facilities work closely with nearby industry to create customized training opportunities.

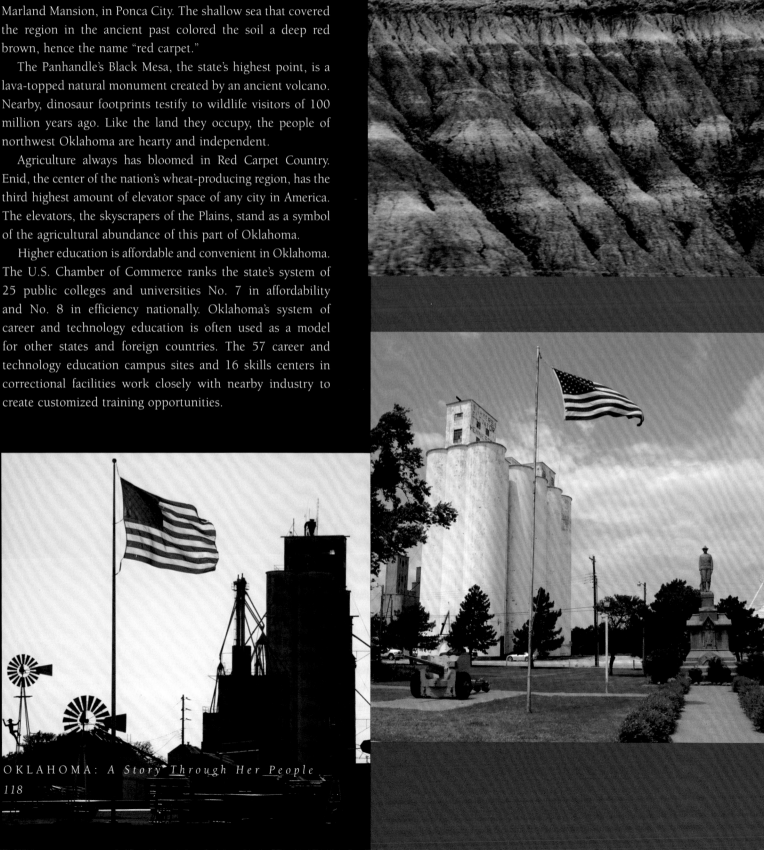

Opposite, top: Northwest Oklahoma.

Opposite, center: Layers depicting the millenniums of change.

Opposite, bottom left: Grain elevator and windmills.

Opposite, bottom right: Farmers Grain elevators in Hennessey.

Above: Wind turbines and crops.

Right: Boys Park.

People Living, Working, and Playing Together

Above and opposite: The Myriad Botanical Gardens in Oklahoma City

6

Residents and visitors alike give Oklahomans standing ovations and acclaim for supporting a variety of arts that advance the state's culture. The state ranks seventeenth in the nation in per capita spending on the arts. With more than 300 museums of fine art, natural history, and science; world-class performing arts; and an abundance of festivals, Oklahoma's culture is a blend of peoples, history, and excellence. The Gilcrease Museum in Tulsa houses the world's largest collection of art of the American West. The offering of museums is as diverse as Tulsa's Philbrook Museum of Art to Oklahoma City's National Cowboy and Western Heritage Museum.

Oklahoma is her people—present and past. Oklahomans have changed the world around them. Oklahoma artists have used oils, pastels, pencils, stone, and many other media to project their imagination in the form of art. In the same way, Oklahoma authors and poets have recorded our past in both fiction and non-fiction. Marquis James won Pulitzer Prizes for biographies of Sam Houston and Andrew Jackson. Grant Foreman wrote of the American West. Angie Debo courageously told the story of the hardships faced by the American Indians being forced to move to Indian Territory. John Hope Franklin became the nation's leading African American historian.

The world of fiction has been enriched by Oklahoma authors with romance, science fiction, and Western novels. Ralph Ellison drew up his childhood in northeast Oklahoma City to write *Invisible Man*, considered one of America's top five novels of the twentieth century. Louis L'Amour wrote than 100 fiction masterpieces. Tony Hillerman, Billie Letts, S. E. Hinton, Merline Lovelace, C. J. Cherryh, Rilla Askew, Michael Wallis, Glenn Shirley, and Carolyn Hart have produced best-selling books, and some have been made into major movies.

Some of the early art in Oklahoma came from artists who traveled with expeditions sent to explore the new land and make a record of its natural resources and people. The American Indian Tribes that were relocated in Oklahoma produced many artists such as Woodrow Crumbo, a Pottawatomie; Jerome Tiger, a Creek-Seminole; and Acee Blue Eagle, the first American Indian artist to embark on a solo career and travel worldwide to promote American Indian art.

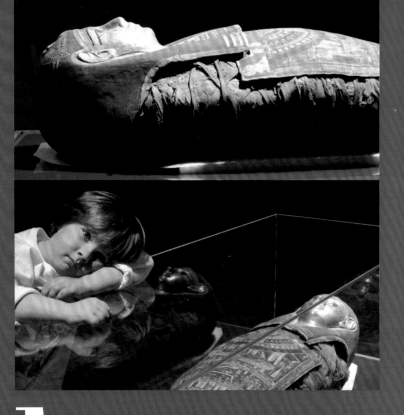

Professor Oscar Jacobson at the University of Oklahoma tutored five young Kiowa art students whose artistic endeavors as the Kiowa Five literally transformed American Indian art. Apache Allan Houser became one of the nation's leading sculptors. Charles Banks Wilson won international acclaim for his paintings, including major works in the Oklahoma State Capitol.

Wilson Hurley added his large-scale murals to the Sam Noble Special Events Center of the National Cowboy and Western Heritage Museum in Oklahoma City. In the past decade, Mike Wimmer of Muskogee has become Oklahoma's most famous modern painter. His landscapes and portraits are displayed in many private and public collections.

Donna Merkt of the Mabee-Gerrer Museum of Art in Shawnee, states:

"The Shawnee CVB and the museum have had a fruitful partnership for over a decade. The staff at the CVB works diligently to promote the museum and their other partners." Merkt, who is the museum's curator of education, added, "The CVB provides strong tourism development for the museum, promoting the museum's activities and events in ads, on their webpage, on social media, in print media and signage, and at tourism events, allowing the museum to focus valuable time and dollars on education, exhibitions, and preservation.

"The CVB is a primary supporter of the annual Arts Trek Festival, which promotes the artists and performers in the Shawnee area. Support from the CVB assisted in getting this festival off the ground, helping it grow from 1,000 visitors in 2010 to 3,000 visitors in 2014," she stated.

-Mike McCormick
Shawnee Convention & Visitors Bureau

Top: *International Finals Youth Rodeo Bull Rider, Shawnee, 2013.*

PHOTOGRAPH COURTESY OF JAMES PFIFER, RODEOBUM.COM.

Center: *International Finals Youth Rodeo Steer Wrestler, Shawnee, 2013.*

PHOTOGRAPH COURTESY OF JAMES PFIFER, RODEOBUM.COM.

Bottom: *International Finals Youth Rodeo, Tie Down Roper, Shawnee, 2013.*

PHOTOGRAPH COURTESY OF JAMES PFIFER, RODEOBUM.COM.

Mike Jackson is operations manager of the Heart of Oklahoma Exposition Center, the largest facility in Shawnee that draws an estimated 15,000 people monthly.

"There are a lot of events they (the Convention & Visitors Bureau or CVB) financially support," Jackson said. Among them are calf roping, barrel racing and others. He also noted the CVB provides welcome bags and information for visitors to the community. "They help with our motels. They help with the International Finals Youth Rodeo, playing a huge role in it." They help with the media for the IFYR, which is considered the richest youth rodeo in the world. This is the twenty-second consecutive year for the event and today provides more than $200,000 in prize money and other awards for the winning contestants.

Jackson also pointed out the CVB helps with large RV rallies, a number of which Farris and Expo staff member Stephanie Gideon help recruit for the Expo and the community. Right after this year's IFYR in July, a 500-unit RV rally will descend upon the Expo Center, and following it will be the National Junior Beefmaster Show with more than 400 head of cattle and contestants from thirteen states attending.

The 2015 Central District Livestock Show, another large event, drew huge numbers of youth and the parents who support them.

Jackson said the National Barrel Horse Association has at least six events annually and the State 4-H Horse Show also was held at the Expo.

-Mike McCormick
Shawnee Convention & Visitors Bureau

OKLAHOMA: *A Story Through Her People*

Due to the leadership and assistance provided by the CVB, in cooperation with local tribal nations, the Jim Thorpe Games came to Shawnee in June 2014. The event drew thousands of folks to the community and surrounding areas. An estimated 1,600 Native athletes converged on our community for the competition held throughout the week of June 8-14. representing more than seventy Native American Nations.

Kinlee Farris spent many hours working with people both locally and outside the city to bring the games here. Bringing the games to Shawnee from Oklahoma City where it's been hosted the past couple of years shows the cooperation it took from many entities and the many hours Farris spent working with them. The games featured eleven sports and this year in addition to those an Oklahoma Native American High School Football Game was held. Among the sports included were tennis, softball, basketball, golf, track and field, cross country, wrestling, stickball exhibition, martial arts, beach volleyball and lacrosse exhibition.

Opening ceremonies for the Jim Thorpe Native American Games, that moved to Shawnee in June 2014.
PHOTOGRAPH COURTESY OF THE SHAWNEE CHAMBER OF COMMERCE.

As Farris explained what really made bringing the games here possible was "Our community stepped up to the plate. Without our partners it would not have been possible." Executive director of the Jim Thorpe Native American Games is Annetta Abbott. Sheelaborated also on what made bringing the games to the Shawnee community possible. "I want to thank Oklahoma Baptist University and we are very excited about the facilities. We were able to play an All-Star football game, track and field, beach volleyball, and basketball here," she said. "Without the partnership that we have formed with Brian Morris and the athletic staff at OBU that would not be possible. One of the key factors in moving the games to Shawnee, was having a place to really host all of the events," she said.

Other key venues for the games included St. Gregory's University, Gordon Cooper Technology Center, FireLake Arena, FireLake Ballfields, Firelake Golf Course, and Shawnee High School. When Farris was approached by Abbott in the fall of 2013 about relocating the games to Shawnee as early as June 2014, Farris took the lead in visiting with the key partners to make the games possible.

An additional benefit to having the games at the various venues in the community is the economic impact. This is just another positive for Shawnee and the community which welcomed the athletes and the people they brought with them.

The Shawnee Trail Days Festival was another new event scheduled right behind the Jim Thorpe Games. The CVB partnered with Safe Events for Families, and the event spanned over parts of three days and two nights.

-Mike McCormick
Shawnee Convention & Visitors Bureau

Opposite, top: Off to the zebra and ostrich races.

Opposite: Center, left and below: Remington Park.

Opposite: Center, right: Wipe-out.

Left: Camels are saddled up!

Bottom, left: Camel racing.

Bottom, right: Remington Park: Racing & Casino.

Elk City

ROUTE US 66

NATIONAL ROUTE 66 MUSEUM

ELK CITY, OK

SALOON

ELK CREEK PALACE FARO TABLES

Opposite page: *The National Route 66 Museum in Elk City is located on Route 66.*

Top: *Getting your kicks on Route 66 Tulsa!*

Above: *Miami, Oklahoma…the gateway.*

Right: *Route 66 roadside attraction—the Blue Whale, in Catoosa.*

ROUTE 66 ROADSIDE ATTRACTION

BLUE WHALE, CATOOSA, OKLAHOMA
Built in the early 1970's as an anniversary gift, the
Blue Whale turned into a swimming park and closed in 1988.

Recognized by Hampton Hotels Save-A-Landmark program as a site worth seeing

People always
have been Oklahoma's
greatest resource.

Above: Induction into the Oklahoma Hall of Fame is the highest honor an Oklahoman can receive from the State of Oklahoma.

15 FT 9 IN

People always have been Oklahoma's greatest resource. Oklahomans have overcome many disasters—both natural and manmade. For the first two decades of statehood, the new state struggled to find its place in the Union. The population grew and the discovery of oil put substantial money into the state treasury. Then, the stock market crashed in 1929 and the Great Depression began.

If falling oil and farm prices were not horrible enough, a searing drought hit the High Plains. Farm foreclosures were daily events. Dust storms took the topsoil from thousands of acres of rich farmland that the drought had baked and cracked. During the Great Depression, Oklahoma lost more than 400,000 of its people as the jobless headed for what they perceived was a better life in western states.

Even though thousands of families left Oklahoma during the Great Depression, most stayed and made the best of a bad situation. Churches and families made sure their neighbors had enough to eat. New Deal programs of President Franklin D. Roosevelt gave jobs to hard-working Oklahomans, and the result was thousands of WPA projects that built schools, national guard armories, city halls, dams, parks, storm cellars, and football stadiums. Three quarters of a century later, many of the structures built by the make-work projects of the Roosevelt administration are still in use.

Oklahoma suffered more than many surrounding states from the ravages of the Great Depression, and it took longer for the state to climb back to economic stability. Historian Angie Debo said, "Oklahomans came out of the Great Depression a stronger people." With a resilience seldom replicated in American history, Oklahomans who stayed, or returned, were determined to make Oklahoma a fine place to live and raise their families. We now call that resolve, **THE OKLAHOMA STANDARD.**

Oklahomans had overcome bad economic times and extreme weather, but had never encountered the sorrow and pain that took place in Oklahoma City on the morning of April 19, 1995. The world watched as first responders found 168 men, women, and children in the rubble of the bombed-out Alfred P. Murrah Federal Building. But, again, the people of the state stood with the victims, helped return the area to normal, and constructed the Oklahoma City National Memorial and Museum.

Opposite: One of the few remaining steel girder bridges left in Oklahoma. It is located in southeastern Oklahoma.

Left: Oklahoma's only covered bridge is in Lexington.

This page: Oklahoma's geographic location is in the eye of Tornado Alley.

Opposite, left column and top: Disaster relief workers immediately rally after devastation caused by tornados—as shown here in Moore, Oklahoma.
This relief crew camped at one of the few remaining structures in that area, which turned out to be a church.
The relief workers set up RVs complete with showers, laundry facilites and food prep. In this case they used the church kitchen and fed both relief workers and storm survivors. Therapy dogs are also brought in.

Opposite, bottom right: St. Anthony's Catholic Church in Okeene.

Because of Oklahoma's geographic location in the eye of tornado alley, the threat of tornadoes has created dread and consternation since the first settlers made their home here. Without warning, tornadoes spread destruction in early Oklahoma. The state's two deadliest tornadoes killed more than 100 people each—in Snyder in 1905 and Woodward in 1947.

As weather forecasters developed ways to provide an advance warning of tornadic activity, lives were saved. After the Woodward tornado in 1947, no extensive loss of life occurred due to tornadoes in Oklahoma for a half century. However, on May 3, 1999, a rash of record-making twisters hit the state. More than seventy tornadoes hit the state within a twelve hour period, the strongest an EF-5, with the strongest winds ever recorded, and killed 48 people and produced more than $1.1 billion in damage.

The **OKLAHOMA STANDARD** again was displayed as neighbors helped neighbors and churches and other community organizations rushed to the rescue. Within weeks, the debris was removed and sounds of hammers and saws rang through the hundreds of square blocks that had been ravaged by tornadoes.

Ironically, the May 3 tragedy was repeated on May 20, 2013, when 24 people were killed and nearly 400 injured when another EF-5 tornado followed a similar track through Moore and caused more than $2 billion in damage. National news anchors rushed to Moore for twenty-four hour coverage of the horrific example of Mother Nature's fury and reported on the courage, good attitude, and resilience of Oklahomans. The world saw what the **OKLAHOMA STANDARD** really was.

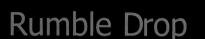

One of the ways that Oklahomans are able to cope with problems is in their extreme love for sports. High school and college football reign supreme in the state. The latest sports craze is the Oklahoma City Thunder, a championship National Basketball Association franchise that plays its home games in the Chesapeake Arena. When the Thunder reached the NBA Finals in 2012, it was near the pinnacle in state sports history, with unprecedented national exposure.

Oklahoma's sports history is unique. One of every ten major league baseball players in the history of the national pastime has an Oklahoma connection. Oklahoma native Jim Thorpe was a legendary Olympic athlete and the first president of the National Football League. Mickey Mantle is among the most recognized names in baseball history. The Oklahoma Sports Hall of Fame in Oklahoma City displays memorabilia from Oklahoma sports heroes.

High schools all over Oklahoma
love and celebrate their sports.

Above: Noble High School band members performing with the Macy's Great American Marching Band at the Macy's Thanksgiving Day Parade in New York City, 2014. Students from other Oklahoma schools were also invited to participate, including the Union High School Band from Broken Arrow and cheerleaders from Lexington. Oklahoma's own actress/singer Kristin Chenoweth, also from Broken Arrow, graced the Macy's Parade that year.

The Oklahoma Military Academy (OMA) that replaced Eastern University Preparatory School (EUPS) in Claremore, closed in 1917. In January 1919 State Representative H. Tom Kight of Claremore introduced legislation calling for the creation of a state-sponsored military school in order that the United States would never find itself ill prepared for war as it had been in 1917. The mood of the country, coupled with the lack of schools in northeastern Oklahoma, led legislators to pass Kight's bill in March 1919.

OMA opened in the fall of 1919 as a secondary school, with curriculum including mandatory vocational and military training for all cadets, beginning with a corps of forty cadets. It grew steadily, becoming a six-year institution in 1923 and offering cadets four years of high school and two years of junior college. More than twenty-five hundred graduates served their country as officers and noncommissioned officers in World War II, Korea, and Vietnam. Six became general-grade officers. More than one hundred OMA men gave their lives.

Despite OMA's successes, enrollments declined in the late 1960s and OMA closed on July 1, 1971. Rogers State College (now University) has occupied the OMA campus from 1971 to today.

Rogers State University

Above: The Rogers State University campus has three large-scale sculptures of U.S. presidents: Thomas Jefferson, George Washington and Abraham Lincoln. The Jefferson statue is near the main entrance of the Claremore campus.

Below: Rogers State University in Claremore.

Langston University

Above and right: Langston University team spirit.

Bottom: The Lions head football coach Dwone Sanders at Langston University.

Oklahoma State University

The four photographs at left, clockwise, starting from the top:

Prentice Gautt, #38, was a running back for the University of Oklahoma from 1956 to 1959.

Head Coach Barry Switzer.

Football Coach Bud Wilkinson is carried off the field, 1954.

Football Coach Bennie Owen at the University of Oklahoma from 1905 to 1926.

Below: Women's basketball team University of Oklahoma .

University of Oklahoma

Clockwise, starting from the top:

The Gaylord Family Oklahoma Memorial Stadium, September 2014.
PHOTOGRAPH COURTESY OF STACY WEST.

The Gaylord Family Oklahoma Memorial Stadium, April 2009.
PHOTOGRAPH COURTESY OF ROBERT H. TAYLOR.

University of Oklahoma softball team and President David Boren on the far right.

Women's NCAA gymnastics champions.

Sooners football team.

Profiles of businesses, organizations, and families that have contributed to the development and economic base of Oklahoma

Oklahoma Partners

Quality of Life

Healthcare providers, school districts, universities and other institutions
that contribute to the quality of life in Oklahoma

SPECIAL
THANKS TO

McCasland Foundation,
Duncan

John "Jack" Smith Zink

When he authored the life story of the legendary Jack Zink in *To Indy and Beyond* (2008), Dr. Bob Blackburn quoted from remarks Jack made at his induction into the Oklahoma Hall of Fame in 1989:

"[It] is an appropriate summary of Jack's life: The man who wins is the man who tries. I hope this book will encourage others to do the same. Jack would want it that way."

The life work of John "Jack" Smith Zink truly epitomizes this concept. Jack tried a lot— and with tremendous success.

A Tulsa native, John "Jack" Smith Zink was born on October 17, 1928, and entered Oklahoma A&M University (now Oklahoma State University) in Stillwater in 1946, where he received a degree in mechanical engineering in 1951.

His passion for racing began in 1937 when he visited the Detroit Motor Speedway with an uncle, and was fueled during countless summer nights learning the names and styles of his favorite drivers back home at the Tulsa Fairgrounds Speedway. He built his first race car in 1941 and fashioned his first dirt race track west of his father's industrial plant on Peoria Avenue in Tulsa. By 1951, Jack had become "one of the most successful drivers on regional dirt tracks [and] was a regular at Taft Stadium in Oklahoma City." Just four years later, Jack and his race team would celebrate the first of two consecutive wins at the Indianapolis 500.

At the same time, Jack began his career "as the only sales engineer" for John Zink Company, which was founded by his father in 1929. It was a position that he took very seriously and a period in which the company was flourishing with new innovations in the combustion field. After he was named president of John Zink Company in the early 1960s, Jack grew the company into an international corporation. Throughout his entire career, he remained dedicated to the field of manufacturing and engineering, authoring thirty-five patents on combustion and other equipment.

Jack was honored with a number of significant awards throughout his life and career in the field. His alma mater, Oklahoma State University, inducted him into its College of Engineering Hall of Fame and awarded him the Henry G. Bennett Distinguished Service Award. He was named Outstanding Business Leader by The University of Tulsa and was honored by the Boy Scouts of America with the Silver Beaver Award for service to youth.

A veteran race car driver, Jack was inducted into the Motor Sports Hall of Fame by the Indianapolis Motor Speedway, and served on the board of directors and was chairman of the engine committee of the United States Automobile Club.

Jack's commitment to his life's work was rivaled only by his dedication to the community. A lifetime supporter of scouting, he served five terms as president of the Indian

Nations Council, Boy Scouts of America, with over 25,000 boys and adult leaders in the council. He also assisted countless other community organizations and served as chairman or president of the Tulsa River Parks Authority, Oklahoma Wildlife Commission, Oklahoma Department of Wildlife Conservation, Tulsa Area United Way, Hillcrest Medical Center Foundation, Oklahoma Foundation for Excellence, Oklahoma Junior Livestock Auction, Tulsa County Fairgrounds Trust Authority, Young Presidents' Organization, and The Tulsa Foundation. He also served on the boards of Telex Corp., Sunbeam Corp., Unit Corp., Matrix Service Corp., First National Bank, and Liberty Bank.

After the death of his father in 1973, Jack and his sister, Jill, joined other family members in working through the John Steele Zink Foundation to "improve the quality of life in their hometown." Healthcare, the arts, education and outstanding community organizations such as the Salvation Army, Oklahoma State University, The University of Tulsa, Philbrook Museum of Art, Gilcrease Museum of Art, Tulsa Area United Way, Boy Scouts of America, and Girl Scouts of the USA received great support.

Among the many outstanding legacies produced through the work of the Foundation is the low-water dam on the Arkansas River at Thirty-first Street in Tulsa. The Foundation pledged $1 million to aid Tulsa's ambitious River Parks Project in the 1970s. The lake created by the endeavor was named Zink Lake by the Tulsa City Council and opened to more than 150,000 visitors on September 3, 1983.

Without doubt, the John Zink Ranch (covered separately in this book) is Jack's fondest legacy. Occupying 33,000 sprawling acres, it has afforded more than a million people a unique use of natural, undeveloped northeastern Oklahoma countryside over the past seventy years, and is poised to continue to do so for decades—even centuries—to come.

Indeed, John "Jack" Smith Zink did try a little bit of everything—engineering, business, racing, philanthropy, and you-name-it in the great out-of-doors. And Jack Zink succeeded—in life—like few men have.

ZINK RANCH

Top: "The Rendezvous" building.

The John Zink Ranch was first envisioned by John Steele Zink. After his company's foundry burned in 1945, John used the settlement from his insurance claim to purchase "a picturesque parcel of land in Osage County" and, for the next sixteen years, gradually bought much of the land around it. John was passionate about the site and began improving it almost immediately. He added a 110 by 160 foot building he christened "The Rendezvous," which included bunk beds and hunting-lodge style furnishings. He later added a state-of-the-art rifle range, which *Precision Shooting* magazine named in 1956 as the "nation's best bench rest shooting range." He built roads and ponds and even a "replica of a frontier boomtown for the Boy Scouts."

Today that original passion and vision remain in the hearts of the Zink family and are lived out across the unique landscape of the Ranch. Following John's death in 1973, his son Jack continued to build the Ranch into "a combination of wildlife preserve, outdoor park, and ever-changing venue for activities as diverse as motorcycle races and bird watching."

Much of the property is home to permanent Boy and Girl Scout camps with outstanding facilities, which are used by tens of thousands of Boy and Girl Scout members, parents, and volunteers every year. The family scouting complex, Cub World, was built to include The Land Ship, The Native American Nature Center, Turkey Creek Village, and King Arthur's Castle. There is also an Aquatics Sports Center at nearby Skiatook Lake. Lodges and cabins for families of scouts offer modern amenities across the Ranch.

The Red Castle Gun Club, with more than 2,000 members, is also situated on the Ranch. Many other groups also use the beautiful hills of Osage County within the Ranch's borders for activities as diverse as motorcycle endurance races, equestrian events, dog tracking, orienteering, bird watching, and a wide variety of other events and activities.

John Steele Zink first purchased 1,800 acres of land for use as the Zink Ranch in 1945. Between then and the time of his death in 1973, he added much acreage to the original purchase. John's son Jack and grandson Darton have followed John's legacy with the addition of more acreage over the years. Today, the Ranch has in excess of 33,000 acres.

John Steele Zink had a vision for the use of the outdoors, and an affinity for scouting in particular. Jack and Darton continued this vision as well, steadily adding and improving facilities at the Ranch for scouting and other users.

The Zink Ranch is nestled among the beautiful, rocky hills in Osage County. Its main entrance is at the intersection of Highway 97 and Rock School Road. While the Ranch does have its own full-time staff, the Boy and Girl Scouts and the Red Castle Gun Club are independently operated and provide staff and programming for their own facilities on the Ranch. Other groups utilize common facilities made available to them by Ranch staff.

Today, the Zink Ranch continues to serve, enhance and preserve this natural habitat. In addition, the Ranch upgrades existing facilities, particularly for the Boy and Girl Scouts, whose mission has been and continues to be well aligned with the philanthropic interests of the Zink family from decades past through present day. The Boy Scouts of America have entered a period of continuous, multiple facilities' enhancements and expansions, and upgrades and additions to Girl Scouts' facilities on the Ranch are currently on the drawing board as well.

The Zink Ranch exists to serve many public interests related to recreation, activities, education, personal development, and general enjoyment of "the great outdoors" on both land and water. The Ranch's expansive facilities and abundant lakefront help facilitate a tremendous variety of activities during all seasons. Of course, scouting is at the head of a long list of Ranch users.

In the fascinating biography, *To Indy and Beyond: The Life of Racing Legend Jack Zink*, Dr. Bob Blackburn writes:

"By 2004, the Zink Ranch meant more to [Jack] than just a home or a retreat from the city and the world of business. It had become more than land and water and woods, more than a place to build roads and buildings and lake. Nothing held a place in his heart like the Ranch. It was a place where people could get close to nature, test themselves, and rediscover the joy of being with friends. For Jack, the Zink Ranch was his gift to the future."

Below: Entry to the Girl Scouts' Camp Swannie.

GATESWAY
FOUNDATION

Above: The rented farmhouse where Helen Gates began providing services for her son Ronnie and his friends.

Below: A large crowd joined Gatesway founder Helen Gates and her close friend Doris Barnes (with shovel) at the groundbreaking of the organization's Broken Arrow headquarters. Among the dignitaries participating in the ceremony were Broken Arrow Mayor Dr. James R. Newcomb (left) and Tulsa Mayor Robert LaFortune (right).

Opening Up the World—these four words truly capture the inspirational story and unforgettable legacy of the Gatesway Foundation, an organization that has remained steadfast through its central focus and driving passion of "opening up the world" to individuals and their families for more than fifty years.

A nonprofit agency providing vocational training, daily care, support and supervision for people who are also intellectually disabled. Gatesway opened its doors as the deeply personal endeavor of its founder, Helen Gates, in 1963. The vision for the Foundation began with the life of Ronnie Gates, Helen's son, who was born in Louisville, Kentucky, in 1933. Ronnie was later diagnosed with Down syndrome by doctors in New York when he was only a few years old.

Devastated by the news as well as the lack of support and facilities that existed across America in the mid-twentieth century for families who found themselves in such a difficult situation, the couple institutionalized Ronnie at Enid State School in northwest Oklahoma.

For the next several years, the family, including Ronnie's younger brother Jack, made the 800 mile trip from Kentucky to Oklahoma. With each visit, Helen soon became concerned that the environment of the school was far less than ideal and worried that Ronnie would ever be able to function in the real world after her death. It was during these difficult years that Helen began an intense study of the topic of vocational rehabilitation and intellectual disabilities, gradually educating herself with courses and certifications in the field.

By the early 1960s, Helen's dream of "having a place for adults with mental disabilities" was becoming a reality. She had successfully formed a flourishing network of families struggling with the same issues as her own, located property and had even secured financial backing for the

construction of a building—and the Gatesway Foundation finally debuted in 1963.

A rented farmhouse along East Seventy-First Street and South Lewis Avenue in Tulsa was the site of the first group home, among only a handful of such facilities at that time in Oklahoma. It was home to six men, including Ronnie.

Over the course of the next decade, government funds as well as help from Tulsa philanthropist Leta Chapman allowed Helen the opportunity to purchase a more spacious property in Broken Arrow. A large home was built at the location, while an education building and vocational training center were eventually added to the campus.

Today, Gatesway continues to encourage families and improve the lives of individuals with disabilities. It is well-known for its Vocational Training Center for those employed in the training center learn valuable skills while doing a variety of tasks, thus creating a workforce that is a genuinely dependable asset to any company. Such work includes assembling, collating, sorting, bagging, boxing, tagging, packaging, shrink wrapping, bundling, labeling, and mail/brochure inserts.

Through federal and state funding initiatives, Gatesway also provides unique vocational services to employers in the community, providing crews of three to five workers and an on-site Employment Specialist. These services may include housekeeping, janitorial, lawn services, delivery and paper-shredding services. The agency strives to match the needs of the employer to the strengths of individuals, creating a mutually beneficial work environment.

The on-campus Training Center at Gatesway provides a variety of jobs on a contract basis that allow every person to learn new vocational skills while earning a paycheck.

Gatesway's vocational rehabilitation program is provided to individuals whose immediate goal is to work independently in the community. It is funded by the Department of Rehabilitation Services supporting individuals to be gainfully employed while building skills and confidence in their own abilities, enabling them to become more independent. Care is taken to secure employment that benefits both the employer and the person served. A trained Employment Consultant matches the skills and desires of the person with the requirements of the employer. Job coaching supports are in place to assist in finding employment and training the worker. In this program, the Employment Consultant gradually fades from the job site over a period of twelve consecutive weeks of employment.

Beyond this far-reaching workforce training program, Gatesway provides a variety of residential options for people with intellectual disabilities. It is one of the only agencies in the State of Oklahoma providing every type of state-approved living option, community residential opportunities, group homes, intermediate care facilities, and adult day services.

The Adult Day Center is a day program designed to provide daily support and supervision to adults with intellectual disabilities. The extensive program is designed for adults eighteen years of age and older and supports the development of friendships and overall quality of life. Each person is encouraged to participate in a variety of activities, while staff members promote inclusion along with choices in educational, recreational, and social activities. The overarching goal at the Center is to stimulate individuals by providing a safe, protective, and enjoyable setting in which they can participate in various activities.

Programs include music therapy, arts and crafts, fun and games, exercise, community activities/awareness, circle of fun, and socialization, and all experienced in a safe environment.

Today, Gatesway serves approximately 400 people with intellectual and developmental needs including Autism, Down syndrome, Fragile X Syndrome, Cerebral Palsy, and Traumatic Brain Injury (incurred before age twenty-one).

In 2012, Gatesway partnered with the Department of Rehabilitation, local high schools and business to introduce the Transition Program, which teaches high school youth with disabilities the skills needed to be independently employed. The students are brought to the classroom nearest their school for half-day training. They then go into the community each day in small groups with highly qualified transition job coaches to volunteer and job shadow at a variety of business. The students explore career options, learn real job skills, make connections to real employers and learn life skills to help them become as independent as possible. In a short time, the program has more

Above: The Gatesway's Annual Balloonfest.

Bottom, left: Gatesway founder Helen Gates poses with her son Ronnie in his room at the newly built Gatesway Foundation.

Bottom, right: Ronnie Gates sits under a portrait of his mother Helen Gates.

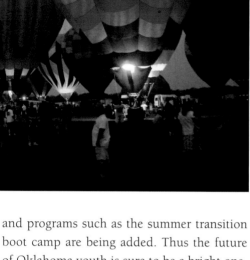

Right: Balloons light up the sky at the Gatesway Foundation's Annual Balloonfest. This yearly fundraising event attracts thousands of visitors each year and assists the agency in promoting its mission of providing opportunities for adults with intellectual disabilities.

Below: Balloon pilots light up the night sky at Gatesway's Annual Balloonfest.

than doubled in size and expanded from one classroom to five reaching into the greater Tulsa and surrounding areas as well as into rural Oklahoma. The Tulsa class has a program for at-risk youth to address the intense needs of these youth. Many of the youth have been or are at risk in areas such as being incarcerated, living in poverty, exposed to gang activity, or teen pregnancy. This program is unique to Gatesway and lives have been set back on course through it. The future for the transition program is exciting as it continues to grow, and new partnerships

and programs such as the summer transition boot camp are being added. Thus the future of Oklahoma youth is sure to be a bright one.

Gatesway CEO Judi Myers, in an interview with *Tulsa People* in late 2013, eloquently describes the foundation, "Helen Gates saw [a] fence between the real world and the world apart, and through her sheer willpower and commitment to making the world a better place, she created a gate. That gate became Gatesway."

For more information about the dynamic work of the Gatesway Foundation, visit the organization online at www.gatesway.org.

Sunbeam Family Services, which began in 1907, provides counseling, early childhood education, foster care and senior service programs to the poor and working poor of Central Oklahoma. All Sunbeam programs and services have been nationally accredited since 1942.

Organized by Mrs. L. D. Swisher and other Oklahoma City women, Sunbeam's object was to serve as a children's home for dependent and neglected children. After fire destroyed its first home in 1912, Sunbeam relocated to 620 Northwest Twenty-first Street, Oklahoma City, where it still has offices. The agency has always relied on the leadership of a strong board of directors, originally consisting solely of women.

Its original purpose included relieving want, providing for the physical comfort, moral elevation, intellectual improvement and general welfare and protection of needy children; purchasing, leasing, renting and controlling real estate needed for its use; and receiving contributions, bequests and donations to carry out its benevolent and charitable work. For almost thirty years, the Sunbeam Home provided entirely institutional care to dependent and neglected children from Oklahoma City and Oklahoma County.

In 1924, Sunbeam became the first children's agency in the ten original agencies in what is today's United Way of Central Oklahoma. Operating a nursery for the children of women working in war-connected industries, Sunbeam also licensed other providers of similar childcare operations during WWII.

Community adult mental health services were added in the post-war 1940s, the only such care in Oklahoma. It has operated a counseling clinic since the late 1930s, and a decade later helped form the Oklahoma Department of Mental Health and Substance Abuse Services. Among the first providers of home-based services for aging adults, Sunbeam continues the Senior Companion Program today.

After 102 years in the same location, the agency will move in late 2014 to Oklahoma City's 1100 Northwest Fourteenth Street, reducing overhead, providing critical services in a safe neighborhood, providing bus stop access and a user-friendly space for children and aging adults, improving access for the physically handicapped, improving work spaces for fuller program integration, and placing all programs and services under one roof.

Sunbeam's 127 employees currently provide fourteen programs, with priority given to children of disadvantage and to low-income aging adults. The agency remains a pacesetter for the United Way of Central Oklahoma.

SUNBEAM FAMILY SERVICES, INC.

DALE ROGERS TRAINING CENTER

Above: Dusty and Dustin Rogers with Waneta, a worker at DRTC in 2013.

"Blazing Trails and Promoting Abilities" is the landmark mission of one of Oklahoma's most celebrated community agencies, the Dale Rogers Training Center (DRTC). The Center has provided more than sixty years of award-winning service to the public and remains the oldest and largest community agency of its kind in the state.

The historic nonprofit organization debuted in 1953 when a group of parents of young children with disabilities formed the Oklahoma County Council for Mentally Retarded Children. The collective dream of these devoted families was to create a place where the children would feel accepted and allowed to learn to and grow at their own pace.

In the same year, Dale Evans Rogers, celebrity and wife of famed cowboy singer and actor Roy Rogers, published the inspiring account of her daughter, Robin, who was born with Down Syndrome and died just before she was two. The book sold millions worldwide and served to open the door to changes for people with disabilities. As a tribute to Dale's life and work, the parents named the school in her honor and soon purchased property on Meek Drive, now Utah Street, where Dale later visited in 1957. They remodeled an old dairy barn on the property to serve as a workshop for older children and began the good fight to raise funds for basic services through what seemed to be an "almost endless" string of rummage sales, pleas for donations, and chili suppers.

As people with disabilities grew older, their needs changed and DRTC began to transition from a school to a vocational training and employment center. After the oil bust, Oklahoma's fiscal pie left a small slice for people with disabilities, and with the economic downturn, the Center had to evaluate what type of nonprofit it wanted to be. The constant goal of the board had remained to "pay our own way" and develop new kinds of jobs and businesses for people with disabilities. Therefore, DRTC realized the best choice to effectively serve people with disabilities was an entrepreneurial approach, which created an entirely unique kind of nonprofit that virtually eliminated annual fundraising campaigns and donor solicitations for cash.

Connie Thrash McGoodwin, the agency's visionary executive director for more than thirty years, reflects on the experience, "We truly wanted our folks to be independent, contributing, tax-paying citizens." As a result, DRTC has become an expert at developing

jobs for people with disabilities, both with the products they manufacture and the services they provide. DRTC changes peoples' lives. It allows some to live independently, to buy cars or homes, to support their families. It offers more than just an income; it offers a sense of pride and accomplishment for people. It integrates individuals with disabilities into the broader society and offers opportunities for social interaction. "I like thinking outside the box and watching the folks we serve earning wages and doing things no one ever thought they could."

Today, DRTC growth and success is unparalleled in Oklahoma. It has evolved into an award-winning, entrepreneurial nonprofit devoted in its support to people with a wide range of disabilities through paid vocational training, in-house programs and work opportunities, as well as competitive community employment.

Its programs have grown beyond the traditional sheltered workshop to include: the special needs program, federal contracts in food and custodial services and unique businesses such as Prism Place Awards and Trophies, Wyman Frame, Prairie Spices

through a specialty gift shop that is also online, and Papa Murphy's Take and Bake Pizza franchise.

DRTC also works in partnership with a variety of community businesses and organizations to provide resources and consultation to other nonprofits and community service providers, offers volunteer and practicum sites for students and mentorship and resources to My Hearts Appeal, a growing nonprofit, which offers education and training opportunities to people with disabilities in Liberia, Africa. DRTC clients also volunteered more than 1,305 hours annually to groups such as the Salvation Army, Litter Blitz, Memorial Marathon, Regional Food Bank, Feed the Children, and Pets and People.

More than 1,200 teens and adults are trained or employed every year, while 83 percent of the Center's revenue is self-generated and 84 percent of its programs are based in the community itself. Professional staff and the Board of Directors work strategically to insure quality and self-sufficiency for people with disabilities. Simply put, DRTC is the expert in developing jobs for people with disabilities, both with the products they manufacture and the services they provide.

DRTC is headquartered at 2501 North Utah in Oklahoma City, with branches in Altus, Norman, Lawton, Midwest City. DRTC can be found online at www.drtc.org.

INASMUCH FOUNDATION

ETHICS AND EXCELLENCE IN JOURNALISM FOUNDATION

Above: Edith Kinney Gaylord.

Below: Left to right, Edith Kinney Gaylord and Eleanor Roosevelt.

Over her lifetime, Edith Kinney Gaylord (1916-2001) supported many organizations and projects, often anonymously. Her interests were diverse, ranging from education and health to the arts and environment. In 1982, she formed two foundations to carry on her giving—Inasmuch Foundation and Ethics and Excellence in Journalism Foundation.

Inasmuch Foundation is dedicated to the betterment of people and the communities and neighborhoods in which they live. It was named after careful consideration by Edith, who selected the word Inasmuch as a reflection of what she wanted the foundation to embody—an institution created to aid all those in our communities. The name was taken from the Gospel of St. Matthew in the King James Version of the Bible, where Jesus expressed, "Inasmuch as ye have done it unto one of the least of these, my brethren, ye have done it unto me."

Today, Inasmuch remains dedicated to that vision. The core of its philanthropy is intended to enrich and enhance the quality of lives it touches; to lessen suffering whenever possible and to strengthen and support institutions and organizations in ways that benefit communities and the individuals served. The foundation assists charitable and educational organizations in achieving their goals and has provided grants to 691 organizations totaling $122.6 million since its inception.

The foundation's involvement in the Oklahoma community remains influential to many of the state's most important programs

for children and families including Oklahoma City Educare, Smart Start Central Oklahoma, Homeless Alliance, Teach for America, John W. Rex Elementary School, ReMerge, and Oklahoma City National Memorial, to name a few.

Beyond her philanthropic endeavors, Edith was a pioneer journalist with a life-long passion for news. She established the Ethics and Excellence in Journalism Foundation (EEJF) in 1982 to support organizations dedicated to advancing the quality and ethical standards of journalism.

Today, the Ethics and Excellence in Journalism Foundation makes grants to journalism schools and other non-profit journalism organizations primarily in the areas of investigative reporting, youth education, and professional development.

Through these grants, EEJF invests in the future of journalism by building the ethics, skills and opportunities needed to advance principled, probing news and information. Gaylord College of Journalism and Mass Communications, Oklahoma Watch, Investigative News Network, Fund for Investigative Journalism, and Friends of the Oklahoma History Center are some of the main grantees of the foundation. In all, EEJF has given over 490 organizations across the United States have received grants totaling more than $37 million.

Inasmuch Foundation and the Ethics and Excellence in Journalism Foundation have a staff of twelve dedicated employees. They are located at 210 Park Avenue in Oklahoma City and online at www.inasmuchfoundation.org and www.journalismfoundation.org.

Above: Gaylord Hall.

Below: Oklahoma City Educare.

YMCA

The Y's four core values are caring, honesty, respect and responsibility. We challenge our members and participants to believe in and behave according to these values. Our core values unite us as a movement with a common cause. They are the shared beliefs and essential principles that guide our behavior, interactions with each other and decision-making.

We believe that to bring about meaningful change in individuals and communities, we must be focused and accountable. That is why we focus our work in three key areas that are fundamental to strengthening community: youth development, healthy living and social responsibility.

At the Y, strengthening community is our cause. Every day, we work side-by-side with our neighbors to make sure that everyone, regardless of age, income or background, has the opportunity to learn, grow and thrive.

The YMCA of greater Oklahoma City was formed in May of 1889, one month after the famous Oklahoma Land Run. In those days, the Y's purpose was to provide a source of strength and positive influence for young men who had traveled far from their families to make a new life for themselves.

The YMCA of Greater Oklahoma City has celebrated 125 years. Today, we have more than 900 full and part-time staff members serving in a wide variety of positions within our 8 branches, 7 programs centers, and 25 community-based program sites. Program and administrative functions are coordinated through the association office. We have grown and changed with the times, providing services and solutions to community problems that impact the population. Financial assistance, teaching children to swim, teen leadership programs and providing school-age childcare are just some of the ways the Y provides for the community.

STRENGTHENING OUR COMMUNITY
FOR *125* YEARS

University of Oklahoma

With the vision and leadership of President David L. Boren, the University of Oklahoma has become a pacesetter in American public higher education. Emphasis on four presidential priorities—teaching quality, research expansion, globalization and creation of community—has propelled the University forward, resulting in a dramatic number of major milestones in the almost twenty years since he assumed the presidency and became OU's second longest-serving president since OU's founding in 1890.

The twenty years since he assumed the presidency have been marked by an emphasis on putting students first. There is not another university president in the country more committed to students as the number one priority. President Boren teaches an American government class each semester and is one of the few presidents of major universities to teach.

He guides the faculty with the belief that while the University has an important role to play in the realm of research, the teaching of students is its central purpose. President Boren believes that the ability to think critically is developed as the two generations come together in the classroom, and that it is through great teaching that intellectual curiosity is awakened and human potential is nurtured.

This focus on student quality and teaching excellence has resulted in OU producing the academically highest ranked student body, the highest graduation rate of any public university in the state and the largest number of degrees conferred of any college or university in Oklahoma.

With more and more of our nation's leaders trained at public universities, President Boren believes that our public institutions must be truly excellent. The proof of OU's academic excellence is the University's No. 1 ranking among all public universities in the number of National Merit Scholars enrolled and OU's achievement this year of being the only public or private university in America to produce a Rhodes Scholar, a Marshall Scholar, a Mitchell Scholar, A Goldwater Scholar, a Truman Scholar and a Fulbright Scholar.

To improve teaching quality, a Presidential Professors Program was instituted in 1995 to revitalize OU's commitment to teaching and to reward outstanding educators. Also, the Retired Professors Programs was established to bring a generation of vital knowledge and experience back into the classroom. Faculty-in-Residence Programs were instituted so that faculty families live in apartments in all major residence halls to bring mentoring and stimulating programs to students.

Underlining the importance of a global education, President Boren has expanded study abroad programs, instituted an Interdisciplinary International Programs Center, created a College of International Studies, established a Religious Studies Program and instituted OU Cousins, a program that pairs American students with international students to share social and informal time together to improve understanding of various cultures. President Boren believes that the U. S. must learn how to better form partnerships with other nations

Bottom left: The South Oval.

PHOTOGRAPH COURTESY OF ROBERT H. TAYLOR.

on a basis of mutual respect and understanding. This means learning more about the cultures, histories, and languages of others. OU has launched study abroad programs at more than fifty locations around the world. The percentage of OU students studying abroad during their university years has gone from two percent, fifteen years ago to twenty-six percent today. OU has had students on campus from over 110 countries studying at OU. Through the International Programs Center, Foreign Policy Conferences have exposed students, faculty, staff and the public by bringing to the campus world leaders, including Margaret Thatcher, Desmond Tutu, Henry Kissinger and Mikhail Gorbachev.

President Boren, along with OU First Lady, Molly Shi Boren, has created a sense of community in which shared values can flourish. At OU, students are encouraged to develop a commitment to civic responsibility and service to community. As part of OU's commitment to civic education, President Boren established the Institute for American Constitutional Heritage, which sponsors Teach-Ins that bring to campus Pulitzer Prize-winning authors and historians and outstanding scholars to discuss different periods in American history. To underline the importance of giving to a purpose higher than oneself, each year, thousands of OU students gather for The Big Event, a daylong service project to address a variety of community needs.

At OU, research complements teaching. The University transformed an empty field into a 271 acre Research Campus that houses academic and research programs in radar technology, meteorology, genetics, energy and the life sciences. The facilities on OU's Research Campus allow businesses and industries to locate and collaborate with University affiliates in an academic setting and further grow and develop Oklahoma's economy.

The success of University's research was underlined recently when OU was awarded the Carnegie Foundation's Very High Research designation, one of the most important measures that distinguish among institutions of higher education. OU is the first public institution in Oklahoma to be awarded this outstanding recognition.

OU's excellence also was recently reaffirmed by the report of OU's accrediting agency, The Higher Learning Commission of the North Central Association of Colleges and Schools, which called OU "one of the country's leading public research universities that is committed to quality in it research, instructional and service missions."

The Great Reading Room.

PHOTOGRAPH COURTESY OF HUGH SCOTT.

BELOW: PHOTOGRAPH COURTESY OF SHEVAUN WILLIAMS AND ASSOCIATES.

OKLAHOMA STATE UNIVERSITY

Above: Old Central.

PHOTOGRAPH BY PHIL SHOCKLEY.

Below: First-day students.

PHOTOGRAPH BY PHIL SHOCKLEY.

The story of Oklahoma State University began on Christmas Eve, 1890, at the McKennon Opera House in Oklahoma's territorial capital of Guthrie when Territorial Governor George W. Steele signed legislation establishing an Oklahoma Agricultural and Mechanical College (OAMC) in Payne County. OAMC's first students assembled for class on December 14, 1891, even though there were no buildings, no books, and no curriculum. The college's first students attended classes in the Stillwater Congregational Church. The original campus consisted of 200 acres of prairie that were donated by four local homesteaders. The college's first six graduates received their diplomas in 1896.

Visitors to the OSU campus often marvel at its beauty and consistency of architecture. Much of the credit goes to legendary president, Henry G. Bennett, who served from 1928-1951. Dr. Bennett's twenty-five year campus master plan envisioned some of the university's

most famous and beautiful structures, including the Edmon Low Library and the OSU Student Union. A new campus master plan is guiding unprecedented construction that is making OSU more competitive in academics and athletics. Starting in the fall of 2008, OSU has opened the new Multimodal Transportation Terminal, the new North Classroom Building, the west end zone of Boone Pickens Stadium, refurbished Old Central, the Donald W. Reynolds Architecture Building, an upgraded Murray Hall, the new Henry Bellmon Research Center, an updated and expanded Student Union, the Sherman Smith Training Center, the Postal Plaza Gallery, the Greenwood Tennis Center and a new outdoor track. And several other major projects are in the works.

OSU grew quite rapidly following World War II. The post-war years were marked by a huge enrollment surge and the development of the "Veteran's Village" living community. The mid-1940s also were a golden era for athletics at Oklahoma A&M. In a ninety day period in early 1945, OAMC teams won the Cotton Bowl, the NCAA championship in wrestling, and the NCAA championship in basketball. The next year, the wrestling and basketball teams repeated as national champions, and the football team won the Sugar Bowl. OSU's success continues today across both men's and women's athletics. The school has won fifty-one NCAA championships to rank fourth in the country and tops in the Big 12 Conference.

By the 1950s the college had grown substantially and in 1957, OAMC became Oklahoma State University for Agriculture and Applied Science. OSU enrollment more than doubled from 10,385 in 1957 to more than

23,000 in the 1980s. Today, there are more than 36,000 students across the OSU system.

As a land-grant institution, OSU is the "people's" university and remains committed to its founding mission of high-quality teaching, research and outreach. Today, under the guidance of President Burns Hargis, OSU is in the midst of record enrollment, record fundraising and a building boom that is transforming the university. OSU announced in April 2013 that it reached its $1 billion Branding Success campaign goal nearly two years early, raising funds for student scholarships, faculty and facilities.

When it comes to outreach, OSU reaches across the state of Oklahoma. It has five campuses: Stillwater, which includes the Center for Veterinary Health Sciences; OSU-Tulsa; OSU-Oklahoma City; OSU Institute of Technology in Okmulgee; and the OSU Center for Health Sciences in Tulsa, which includes the OSU Medical Center. OSU also boasts nearly twenty agricultural experiment stations statewide, extension offices representing all seventy-seven counties, a sensor testing facility in Ponca City, and a biosciences institute in Ardmore in partnership with the Noble Foundation.

With more than 350 undergraduate and graduate degrees and options, as well as professional degree programs in medicine and veterinary medicine, OSU and its nine different colleges provide unmatched diversity of academic offerings.

Research is the third cornerstone of the university's land-grant mission and OSU's interdisciplinary work across virtually every field of study enhances Oklahoma's economy and its quality of life.

Although OSU is a large, comprehensive university, its size does not minimize the personal attention given to each student. OSU encourages all new students to identify the college in which they wish to major. Because the average number of students majoring in any one department is less than 150, the student can count on personal attention in a friendly environment.

OSU offers students many distinct advantages. It has more than two million volumes in the library; modern research laboratories and equipment; excellent physical education, recreation and student union facilities; nationally recognized residence halls; outstanding cultural events; and nearly forty nationally affiliated fraternities and sororities that provide a stimulating educational and social environment.

From six graduates in 1896, to nearly 5,000 annually today, the small college on the prairie has grown and prospered far beyond the dreams of its founders. OSU teaching, research, and graduates are making a bigger impact on the lives of people around the world than ever before.

Above: OSU Microbiology Lab.
PHOTOGRAPH BY GARY LAWSON.

Below: Boone Pickens Stadium.
PHOTOGRAPH BY PHIL SHOCKLEY.

CANADIAN VALLEY TECHNOLOGY CENTER

The reaction of any individual or entity to a serious problem is a measure of its worth. When a tornado made a direct hit and destroyed all nine buildings of Canadian Valley Technology Center's El Reno Campus on May 31, 2013, the staff, students, and the public reacted immediately. This campus, one of three in the system, was located three miles east of El Reno on Historic Route 66. It was the end of the school term, and the fifteen people on campus sought shelter in a basement classroom. They survived the largest tornado on record—2.6 miles wide and packing winds of 296 m.p.h.—with no one on campus hurt. The campus is being rebuilt and the new buildings will include safe rooms to accommodate 1,200—the number of students, staff and visitors who might be there at any one time.

Canadian Valley Technology center is a career training facility that provides full-time and short-term career and technology training to anyone who lives in the district. Students under the age of twenty-four who live in the district have the opportunity to attend classes tuition free.

This publicly funded center, formerly Canadian Valley Vo-Tech, is part of the Oklahoma Department of Career and Technology Education system. In addition to the El Reno facilities, its other campuses are located in Chickasha and Yukon, offering both daytime and evening classes for high school students and adults. The Business and Industry Services division also provides customized training for area companies.

Its history dates back to the late 1960s, when high school administrators, primarily in Canadian and Grady Counties, sought a way to provide vocational training in areas such as auto mechanics, computers, nursing and welding for high school students. Lacking both the facilities and the funding to do so on-site, they pursued a bond election to fund a centrally located vocational school. The facility would provide a pipeline of skilled workers for jobs not requiring a college education, though many of the school's graduates attend college now. In the words of Dale Hughey, Oklahoma's first vo-tech coordinator, Canadian Valley would provide an "opportunity to learn and earn more quickly."

The school opened in August of 1970, with campuses in El Reno and Chickasha. J. R. Gililland had been hired two years earlier as its first superintendent. Earl Cowan, originally a welding instructor, was named as an administrator and, in 1984, as the superintendent. He succeeded Dr. Roy Peters, who left Canadian Valley to become associate director, then director of the state's vo-tech education agency. The Yukon campus, which opened in 2008, was named in Dr. Cowan's honor.

School safety is a priority of Dr. Greg Winters, the fourth Canadian Valley superintendent. In 2012 the board of education approved almost $11 million in expansion and upgrades at the Chickasha Campus. The addition is named for Assistant Superintendent George M. Tiner, who served the district for almost forty years before retiring in 2013. It includes a safe room to accommodate all students, staff and visitors in case of severe weather. Winters, who has said he wants Canadian Valley Technology Center schools to

be the safest anywhere, has pledged never to build a facility without safe rooms.

He met the challenge of the El Reno campus destruction with a vow that no job would be lost and that school would start on time in August. During that summer, employees and programs assigned to El Reno were temporarily relocated to the Cowan site. The district then leased a 93,000 square foot vacated car dealership in Yukon to serve as home to most of the El Reno campus' relocated programs.

In April of 2014 voters approved a $12 million bond issue to bridge a funding gap between the insurance payout and rebuilding costs. The new construction is to be completed by the summer of 2016.

"Our goal is to prepare people to succeed through quality career and technical education programs and services," Winters says.

Many students perform community outreach and service, including work on Habitat for Humanities homes, donations to the Make-A-Wish Foundation, an HVAC upgrade at the Union City police headquarters, and a disc golf course at Wild Horse Park in Mustang. Staff and students in Chickasha donate time annually for the community's largest holiday event, the Festival of Light.

GORDON COOPER TECHNOLOGY CENTER

Above: Astronaut Gordon Cooper.

Real-world learning at Gordon Cooper Technology Center offers adults and high school students many pathways to success in a range of careers.

Career-focused training from experienced instructors prepares students for success in areas such as nursing, aviation maintenance, advanced manufacturing and many other career fields. Seasoned professionals in GCTC's Business and Industry Services division respond to the needs of retail and manufacturing clients with innovative business solutions, setting them up for success.

The Gordon Cooper Technology Center district covers more than 1,600 square miles in parts of eleven counties including most of Pottawatomie, Seminole, and Lincoln Counties.

The Gordon Cooper Technology Center story began the evening of August 2, 1966, during a meeting called by Senator Ralph Graves at the request of area educators. Fifty school leaders from thirteen communities participated in the initial meeting.

On November 1, 1967, Bill Weaver of Shawnee was elected president of the new vo-tech district school board. Weaver was an influential community leader and general manager of KGFF Radio in Shawnee for thirty-three years. John Paul Brown of Dale, was named vice president; and Doyle Greer of Prague, clerk, along with members John Marshall of Seminole; and Raymond Moon of New Lima. The new board approved naming the tech center in honor of Astronaut Gordon Cooper, a Shawnee native who was a pioneer of space exploration.

On July 1, 1968, Dr. John C. Bruton was named the first superintendent. A formal groundbreaking ceremony at the I-40 and Highway 18 school construction site was held in November 1968 with Congressman Tom Steed as the main speaker. An elaborate dedication ceremony was conducted June 7, 1970. A six-inch wide, red ribbon, which extended all the way around the five original school buildings, was cut to mark the occasion by dignitaries including Astronaut Gordon Cooper.

Today, Gordon Cooper Technology Center continues to build on this legacy, committed to being the premier provider of workforce training and business services in east central Oklahoma. GCTC strives for excellence to keep the school accountable and to empower people, develop thriving families, vibrant communities, and increase economic prosperity for everyone in the district.

Tonkawa, Oklahoma's people and heritage play a significant role in the development of Northern Oklahoma College. After the 1893 Cherokee Strip Land Opening, the government provided school lands as it had done after other openings. From the beginning there was much interest in higher education.

The history of NOC began in 1901 when the Honorable James Wilkin realized the need for a secondary school in the Tonkawa area. After significant political efforts, the Sixth Territorial Legislature passed an appropriation bill on March 1, 1901 for the establishment of the University Preparatory School at Tonkawa. The doors opened to 217 students and seven faculty members.

During the first two decades, the school served as a feeder institution for the University of Oklahoma and paralleled the university curriculum of music, foreign languages, business, literature and military science. The school served as an educational center for the cultural and performing arts, a distinction that continues today with the Kinzer Performing Arts Center and the Renfro Center.

In June 1999, Northern purchased the former Phillips University campus in Enid to expand public educational offerings. The Bridge program, a partnership with Northwestern Oklahoma State University, was developed to encourage smooth transfer for students.

NOC also played a large role in the development of the University Center in Ponca City, providing administration services and course offerings beginning in 1999.

In August 2003, NOC joined in a partnership with Oklahoma State University to create the Gateway Program in Stillwater, which expands opportunities for students who want to meet admission requirements to OSU after successfully completing twenty-four credits at NOC.

Northern is the leader among Oklahoma colleges in technological advances in developing online and interactive television courses that serve students in rural and remote areas who could not otherwise attain a college degree.

Northern Oklahoma College offers an affordable, quality education. Northern offers choices to students who select the place, price and programs that fit their lives. Alumni become learners, earners and leaders prepared to transfer and pursue additional degrees or enter the workforce.

The students, faculty and staff give the three campuses distinct character and they are making a difference to the thousands who achieve their goals at Northern. Northern Oklahoma College creates life-changing higher education experiences for students.

Currently, construction of additional residence halls on the Tonkawa and Enid campuses marks another milestone in Northern's history of providing the best living and learning environment to assist students in reaching their career goals.

Today, Northern serves approximately 5,000 students. For the third consecutive time, the college has been selected by the Washington-based Aspen Institute as one of the top 150 community colleges in the nation and the only one selected in Oklahoma.

Northern Oklahoma College

Central Hall was the first and only building on the Tonkawa campus until 1906. Although construction was authorized in 1901, Central was not occupied until fall classes began in September 1902. The building was (and still is) brick and limestone and originally had a cupola or "belfry-type steeple" and final cost was $23,000. It has four stories. All classes were taught in Central the first four years. Today, Central Hall is now devoted to the Language Arts Division; i.e., English composition, Oral Communication, Mass Communications (journalism and radio broadcast), Developmental Reading, KAYE-FM The Source college radio station and The Maverick college newspaper office.

CITY OF PAULS VALLEY

With a population of 6,012, Pauls Valley, Oklahoma, would be considered relatively small by many people. Its dedicated citizens and leaders work daily to dispel that idea, however. They have achieved remarkable success at fulfilling their vision of being "much more than an ordinary small town." This is due in part to their approach, which combines respect and support for the changing needs of customers, their representatives and employees, along with a total commitment to ethics, integrity, pride and hard work.

Pauls Valley focuses on developing the highest quality, competitively priced and efficiently delivered services to its customers and on improving the quality of life for residents through community partnerships. Pauls Valley, which is located on Interstate 35, is a crossroads between Highways 77 and 19. It utilizes its location and resources to improve economic conditions and raise the area's standard of living. The city, founded in 1857, is the county seat of Garvin County, which has a population of 339,258. Its name honors Smith Paul, who settled in this fertile Washita River Valley in 1857.

Agricultural production adds a gross total of $152 million annually to the economy of Garvin County, with over $42 million of that amount derived from crops. The county ranks first in South Central Oklahoma for its 32,000

acres of wheat, plants 3,300 acres to corn and 8,500 acres to soybeans and is third in Oklahoma for alfalfa and other hay crops. The large quantity of high-quality alfalfa produced here is important to dairy farmers in both Oklahoma and Texas. Garvin County also ranks in the state's top ten for livestock production, with about $105 million in annual sales.

The City of Pauls Valley is named for Smith Paul, who left his home in South Carolina as a young man and found a home with a Chickasaw Tribe in Mississippi. He found work there with the Reverend McClure, a white man who in 1857 had married a Chickasaw lady, Alateecha (Ellen) along the fertile Washita River. As more of the Indians and intermarried whites moved to Paul's Valley, the settlement boasted a stage stop, general store and log homes, all located about a mile south of the present depot museum.

A very early U.S. post office established in Oklahoma Territory was located in Pauls Valley. Sam Paul, Smith's son, was instrumental in the Santa Fe Railroad's decision to locate its line through Pauls Valley in 1887, leading to growth of the new town around the railroad tracks and depot. In 1893 the construction of brick buildings began, and two years later a federal courthouse was built. Pauls Valley was the site in 1899 of Oklahoma's first white school, which was constructed prior to Oklahoma statehood in 1907. Brick streets, built in 1909, are still in use in Pauls Valley today.

Pauls Valley is home to Field's Pecan Pie's production plant. This company proudly boasts a ninety year tradition of making the "World's Best" pecan pies, along with German chocolate, lemon chess and pumpkin pies. These are sold in grocery stores across Oklahoma and in surrounding states.

The Pauls Valley Arts Council operates from the community's Arts and Culture Center, which is housed inside the first city hall and fire station, built in 1919. It offers varied cultural events in keeping with its mission of community enrichment through the arts. Its projects have

Iris Greenwell

included a series of summer concerts in the historic Wacker Park band shell, musical productions and many unique art shows. In 2012 the arts council received Keep Oklahoma Beautiful's Environmental Excellence and Innovation Award, presented by OGE Energy Corp., for their Trash In Fashion Show. The Garvin County Community Living Center and Pauls Valley Recycling Center are also striving to keep Pauls Valley clean and beautiful. In 2013 the Garvin County Community Living Center opened Pauls Valley's first recycling center. During the center's first year of operation, 566,140 pounds of waste were reclaimed, processed and shipped out for recycling.

Numerous recreation and leisure activities for all ages and varied interests are available to Pauls Valley residents and visitors. The 36,540 square foot Donald W. Reynolds Recreation Center, which opened in 2011 through a grant from the Donald W. Reynolds Foundation, is open to all ages. Its gymnasium provides facilities for youth and adult basketball and volleyball; an indoor running/walking track; a well-equipped weight/cardiovascular area; a multipurpose room that is open for rental; and an area specifically designed for aerobics, spin class, yoga, dance, Pilates, and martial arts programs. Other amenities include a room for birthday parties, an indoor playground and a babysitting area.

Two community recreational facilities, the Bosa Indoor Swimming Pool and the Bosa Community Center, are named for Colonel William Bosa, whose goal was to make them available for use over many years. The 12,000 square foot community center, which opened in 1996, features a banquet hall seating 450, and accommodates conferences and other public events, including drama productions, fairs, wedding receptions and large-scale parties. The pool offers water fitness classes, arthritis aquatic programs, lap swimming, open family swim, lifeguard classes, swimming lessons and private party rentals.

The park serves as a playground for all residents and tourists in the community. Its facilities include playground equipment, a band shell, softball and baseball fields, the Rotary club rose garden, tennis courts, a pavilion, a senior citizen center, rodeo grounds and stands, the Garvin County fair facility, football field, basketball gym and a recreational center.

Above: The Donald W. Reynolds Recreation Center.

Below: Rotary International Park.

Okie Noodling Tournament, Heritage Days Rodeo and a Fourth of July Spectacular featuring a championship watermelon seed spitting contest, along with fireworks and patriotic music. Perhaps what Pauls Valley is best known for is the world famous Okie Noodling Tournament and the world's only museum devoted to toy and action figures.

In 2001, then OU student, now Austin-based film director Brad Beasley, partnered with local hand fishermen to document the sport of noodling via a noodling tournament. The original tournament was hosted at the historic Bob's Pig Shop, and just a few hundred people turned out for that evening's weigh-in of the fish. The tournament exceeded expectations over the past fifteen years and moved to Pauls Valley's Wacker Park to accommodate the 10,000 spectators that attend each year. This all day event features live music, food and craft vendors and the Ms. Okie Noodling Pageant. In 2012, it won a Redbud Award for Outstanding Event in the state at the Oklahoma Governor's Conference on Tourism.

Above: Pauls Valley Water Park.

Below: The 1907 Centennial Steamer.

Nestled in the heart of Wacker Park, is the Pauls Valley Water Park. This one-of-a-kind, family aquatic facility features lap lanes, a diving board, lazy river, zero entry children's arena, open and closed flume slides, and south-central Oklahoma's only giant bowl slide.

Pauls Valley remains one of the few Oklahoma stops for Amtrak's passenger train, the *Heartland Flyer.* Many train passengers make Pauls Valley their destination for unique festivals and special events such as Brickfest,

©www.peterjordanphoto.com *"Pauls Valley's 1907 Centennial Steamer"*

In the heart of Pauls Valley's historic downtown sits the Toy and Action Figure Museum. This one-of-a-kind destination has hosted visitors from every state and over forty countries. With group tours provided daily, the museum has seen over 50,000 visitors since it opened its doors. The Toy and Action Figure Museum features over 13,000 action figures, prototypes, behind-the-scenes displays and an interactive area for kids. It has won several awards, including the 2006 Redbud Award for Best New Tourist Attraction in the state, presented at the Oklahoma Governor's Conference on Tourism.

Other outstanding leisure activities available in Pauls Valley include two different games of golf. The nine-hole Pauls Valley City Golf Course, located a half-mile east of I-35 and Exit 70 South, features bent grass greens and Bermuda fairways. It offers a driving range and practice area, as well as a pro shop and snack bar. The Pauls Valley 18-hole disc golf course offers a different sort of golfing challenge that is a growing national pastime.

The rich historical heritage of Pauls Valley is highlighted at the Santa Fe Depot Museum and Plaza. This unique museum is home to a variety of artifacts from the city's founder, Paul, and also includes an authentic steam engine and caboose recognizing Pauls Valley's railroad history. Facilities are available there for meetings, programs, weddings and parties.

Outdoor family fun ranging from camping and fishing to water sports can be found at the Pauls Valley City Lake, which also has a pavilion for reunions or other gatherings. This lake, constructed primarily for water supply

purposes, offers 750 acres of prime fishing. It is home to various species of catfish, crappie, black bass and saugeye. Camping facilities range from full hookups to primitive camping. Longmire Lake provides another prime spot for fishing, boating, camping, hiking, bird watching, hunting and swimming. It has been designated as a trophy bass lake, with aid from the Oklahoma Wildlife Department, which has monitored the Florida bass stocked there on a semi-annual basis since 1990. This lake is also a favorite wintering habitat for bald eagles, and has hosted as many as a dozen of the regal birds at one time.

For over ninety years the same family has operated Pauls Valley's Royal Twin Theatre, just west of the Santa Fe Depot Plaza Tower Clock. This long-standing piece of Pauls Valley's history houses the town's state-of-the-art digital movie theater, complete with two show rooms, a balcony, concessions and theater seating.

As a mid-point between major cities, Oklahoma City and Dallas, this community offers countless amenities, rich Oklahoma history, ideal location, and unique tourist attractions, making Pauls Valley an excellent place to live, work and play! For more information on this great community, check out www.paulsvalley.com.

Above: The Toy and Action Figure Museum.

Below: Okie Noodler Dave Baggett.

CITY OF STROUD

"The history of this town reads like a fairy tale."–so said the March 11, 1898 issue of the *Stroud Star* newspaper. Like all fairy tales, Stroud has had its share of challenges and setbacks; yet for every villain there has been a hero, and every loss has been met with the drive to recover and thrive. The school mascot is the tiger, yet the phoenix could apply for the position as Stroud is indeed a city that always rises from the ashes of loss and continues to grow toward the future.

Above: Rock Cafe, established 1936.

Below: Main Street, Stroud, on Historic Route 66.

Economic growth has always been a priority for the community. Following the opening of Sac and Fox Nation lands for settlement in 1895, the men of Stroud widened roads and hauled a cotton gin from Guthrie to Stroud over forty miles of bridgeless country. When the Ozark Trail (forerunner to Route 66) was plotted to travel through Stroud, the citizens worked to again widen the roads and some of the stone was used to build the world famous Rock Café and local homes.

When news broke in 1898 that the new railroad would bypass Stroud, the entire town was moved to the railroad, one house at a time, by teams of oxen, horse and mules; all while business continued inside the stores. Every time a challenge has arisen, Stroudites have dealt with the current crisis, rebuilt and moved forward. When a tornado destroyed the Tanger Mall in 1999, Stroudites chose to focus on the future and build new infrastructure for the future instead of dwelling on the current misfortune.

Quality of life has always been important. In 1903 a rapidly growing Stroud had an opera, 2 schools, 5 cotton gins, 2 newspapers, 9 saloons, 11 hotels, 7 livery stables, and numerous churches and stores. With the growth, there was a need for improved infrastructure and city leaders added amenities as they became available, including water wells, which were eventually replaced by beautiful Stroud Lake; gas for heating; electricity; paved roads; and telephones.

This continued lifestyle improvement, as well as being located on Interstate 44, Highway 99 and Route 66, has attracted many people and companies to Stroud. Several companies have worldwide distribution lines including: Mint Turbines, remanufacturer of turbine engines for helicopters and airplanes; John Cassidy Company, distributor of oil field equipment; Miller Truck Lines, transporter of freight; Service King, manufacturer and distributor of oil field equipment; TIMCO, rebuilder of rail cars and servicer of the oil industry with hydrochloric acid, and the Sac & Fox Tribal Nation are poised to grow in the future from tourism to new industry.

Stroud is also a planned destination for international and domestic tourist along "America's Highway"—Route 66, with dining and photo opportunities at the Historic Rock Café and beautiful Stableridge Winery.

STROUD CHAMBER OF COMMERCE

The history of Stroud does read like a fairy tale—yet the story is far from over. Ever since the town was moved to its new location in 1898, Stroud has been known as a place of new beginnings, opportunity, and development.

Indeed that positive attitude has been the launching point of the current growth and development. New infrastructure—both above and below the ground is being installed including new roadways, smart meters for water and electric, new water lines, underground electric lines and improved wireless service.

Following the concept of "begin with what you have," city leaders have focused on the historic economic drivers of Stroud—Agriculture, Oil, Railroad and Education. These keystones are still relevant to Stroud's economy but they have adapted to the needs of the twenty-first century. Agriculture is seen in the wineries and vineyards giving Stroud the honor and distinction of being "Oklahoma's Winery and Grape Capitol," and the Farmers Market. Oil is represented by locally manufactured mobile drilling rigs and the oil storage tank farm in the Industrial Park. The rail line between OKC and Tulsa will include passenger service as well as freight. The 900 students in Stroud Schools take core classes, enrichment programs and extra curricular activities while preparing for careers in college or the workforce. Work ready skills training is provided at Central Technology Center in nearby Drumright.

Even visitors have noticed the expansion at the Stroud Airport, city parks, and Stroud Lake. The airport now hosts fuel pumps with private hangars coming soon. Stroud parks have seen improvements in their baseball/softball fields, public swimming pool, playgrounds, and the installation of the Stroud Skate Park. Stroud Lake is being groomed to become Oklahoma's premier lakeside resort and a major component of the local economy.

The Stroud Chamber of Commerce strives to improve our quality of life with seasonal festivals including the Wine Festival, City Wide Garage Sale, Trick or Treat on Main Street and the Christmas Parade. The newest chamber sponsored project is Stroud Arts, which will establish an arts district, training in various arts media, sponsor displays and performances.

Our development includes regional partnerships as Stroud has become a "Certified Healthy Oklahoma Community" through the Department of Health, continues its clean-up program with "Keep Oklahoma Beautiful," and participates in the OSU and USDA sponsored "Stronger Economies Together" program for regional growth.

Currently, there are 2.3 million people living within sixty miles of Stroud. We hope that many of them will see our vision for the future and become a part of Stroud's culture of pride and partnership. Stroud—come grow with us.

Above: The annual Historic Route 66 Wine and Food Festival.

Below: Stroud Industrial Park, 2014.

SHAWNEE CONVENTION & VISITORS BUREAU

by Mike McCormick

Below: International Finals Youth Rodeo.
PHOTOGRAPH COURTESY OF RODEOBUM.COM.

Bottom: Mabee-Gerrer Museum of Art—Arts Trek!

Tourism is alive and well in Shawnee and Pottawatomie County. Statistics show that dollars spent by tourists provide a significant economic impact regionally and throughout the state. Behind the oil and gas industry and agriculture, tourism is ranked as the third leading industry in Oklahoma. One of the biggest reasons tourism is doing well in Shawnee and Pottawatomie County is because of the Shawnee Convention & Visitors Bureau. Its executive director is Kinlee Farris, a seasoned veteran of the tourism industry.

Shawnee Convention & Visitors Bureau was born in late 1994 when voters in Shawnee agreed to a modest hotel/motel tax of $1 a night per room, including those staying in RVs overnight as well. Several years later community leaders realized the revenue from that small tax was not sufficient to support the type of growth which could be realized with additional revenue. Voters were asked, and they agreed, to increase that to a rate of five percent. The community has not looked back since, and has experienced exponential growth over the past decade.

Mike Jackson is operations manager of the Heart of Oklahoma Exposition Center, the largest facility in Shawnee drawing an estimated average of 15,000 people monthly.

"There are a lot of events they (the CVB) financially support," Jackson said. Among them are calf roping, barrel racing and others. The CVB also provides welcome bags and information for visitors. "They help with our motels. They play a huge role with the International Finals Youth Rodeo." They help with the media for the IFYR, which is considered the richest youth rodeo in the world. 2014 was the twenty-second consecutive year for the event that provides more than $200,000 in prize money and other awards for the winning contestants.

Jackson also pointed out the CVB helps with large RV rallies, a number of which Farris and Expo staff member Stephanie Gideon help recruit. Right after 2014s IFYR in July, a 500-unit RV rally descended upon the Expo Center, and following it was the National Junior Beefmaster Show with more than 400 head of cattle and contestants from thirteen states attending. The 2014 Central District Livestock Show was another large event, drawing huge numbers of youth and parents. Jackson said the National Barrel Horse Association has at least six events annually and the State 4-H Horse Show also was held at the Expo.

Donna Merkt of the Mabee-Gerrer Museum of Art in Shawnee echoed Jackson's remarks. "The Shawnee CVB and the museum have had a fruitful partnership for over a decade. The CVB works diligently to promote the museum and their other partners." Merkt, the museum's curator of education, added, "The CVB provides strong tourism development for the museum, promoting the museum's activities and events in ads, on their webpage, on social media, in print media and signage, and at tourism events, allowing the museum to focus valuable time and dollars on education, exhibitions, and preservation. "The CVB is a primary supporter of the annual Arts Trek Festival, promoting artists and performers in the Shawnee area. Support from the CVB assisted in getting this festival off the ground, helping it grow from 1,000 visitors in 2010 to 3,000 visitors in 2014," she stated.

Due to leadership and assistance provided by the CVB, in cooperation with local tribal nations, the Jim Thorpe Games came to Shawnee in June 2014. The event drew thousands to the community and surrounding areas. An estimated 1,600 Native athletes, representing more than seventy Native American Nations, converged on our community for the competition held throughout the week of June 8-14.

Farris spent many hours working with people both locally and outside the city to bring the games here from Oklahoma City where it has been hosted the past couple of years. It shows the cooperation it took from many entities and the many hours Farris spent working with them. The games featured eleven sports and in 2014 an Oklahoma Native American High School Football Game was added. Among

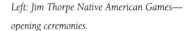

the sports included were tennis, softball, basketball, golf, track and field, cross country, wrestling, stickball exhibition, martial arts, beach volleyball and lacrosse exhibition.

As Farris explained what really made bringing the games here possible was "Our community stepped up to the plate. Without our partners it would not have been possible." Executive director of the Jim Thorpe Native American Games, Annetta Abbott, elaborated also on what made bringing the games to Shawnee possible. "I want to thank Oklahoma Baptist University. We were very excited about the facilities. We were able to play an All-Star football game, track and field, beach volleyball, and basketball here," she said. "Without the partnership that we have formed with Brian Morris and the athletic staff at OBU that would not be possible. A key factor in moving the games to Shawnee was having a place to really host all of the events," she said.

Other key venues for the games included St. Gregory's University, Gordon Cooper Technology Center, FireLake Arena, FireLake Ballfields, Firelake Golf Course, and Shawnee High School. When Farris was approached by Abbott in the fall of 2013 about relocating the games to Shawnee as early as June 2014, Farris took the lead in visiting with the key partners to make the games possible. An additional benefit to having the games at the various venues in the community is the economic impact. This is just another positive for Shawnee and the community that welcomed the athletes and the people they brought with them.

The Shawnee Trail Days Festival was another new event scheduled right behind the Jim Thorpe Games. The CVB partnered with Safe Events for Families, and the event spanned over parts of three days and two nights.

Sherri Rogers is executive director of Frontier Country Marketing Association encompassing twelve counties including Pottawatomie, Lincoln, Seminole, Cleveland, Canadian, Grady, Hughes, Logan, McClain, Okfuskee, Oklahoma and Payne. According to figures recently provided by Rogers, from the Economic Impact of Travelers in Oklahoma Counties, $3.1 billion is generated from those counties.

The efforts of the CVB and its community partners help generate significant economic impact through tourism:

- Pottawatomie County expenditures totaled $75.97 million, ranking it thirteenth in the state.
- The payroll generated from travel expenditures in central Oklahoma exceeded $850 million. Pottawatomie County payroll expenditures at $8.84 million.
- More than 36,000 people are employed in central Oklahoma's travel industry.
- Pottawatomie County employs more than 550 people related to the tourism industry.
- Pottawatomie County's 2012 local tax receipts exceeded $1.38 million.
- State tax receipts annually exceed $170 million from central Oklahoma counties.
- More than $87 million was received in local tax revenue by the twelve central Oklahoma counties.
- During 2012, domestic travelers spent a total of $7.2 billion in Oklahoma. Leisure travelers spent more than $4.7 billion or 66 percent of the total, while business travelers spent $2.4 billion.
- Among the $7.2 billion in leisure travel spending, $5.2 billion (72.8 percent) was spent by non-Oklahoma resident travelers, while 27.2 percent was attributable to Oklahoma resident travel in state.

Bottom Line: tourism remains strong in this area and most of it can be attributed to the efforts of the local Conventions & Visitors Bureau in cooperation with other entities.

CITY OF WOODWARD

A colorful history and emphasis on a strong economy and improvements to the quality of life for its citizens define today's Woodward, Oklahoma. Originally the home of Kiowa, Apache, Cheyenne, Comanche and Arapahoe Tribes, the town was established in 1887, as a siding on the Southern Kansas Railway. It soon became an important shipping point, provisioning Fort Supply and loading cattle for shipment to the east.

Opening of the Cherokee Outlet in 1893 led to a deserved reputation as a wild and wooly town. At one time twenty-three saloons and fifteen brothels were numbered among its businesses. Woodward was the site of the famed "Soiled Dove" trial in which Sam Houston's youngest son, Temple Lea Houston, successfully defended a hopelessly guilty prostitute. After Temple's impassioned closing argument, the jury deliberated just ten minutes before acquitting his client.

Oklahoma was admitted to statehood in 1907, and in the years since has achieved what a resident once described as "the town you've been wishing for, dreaming of, and looking for." The seat of government for Woodward County, the City of Woodward enjoys a thriving economy and low unemployment.

It lies in an oil and natural gas area of the Anadarko Basin, and has enjoyed significant growth since discovery of natural gas in the county. One of the world's largest deposits of iodine also lies underground in Woodward County, leading a number of companies to explore for and produce crude iodine here.

"Our status as a major focus of the energy industry has been enhanced by the addition of alternative energy solutions such as Wind Power Generation, totaling a regional energy investment of $2 billion," City Manager Alan Riffel said. "We are now leading the way in 'green' technology with over 450 wind-powered turbines lining the hills of Woodward, generating power and employing hundreds in the area."

Agriculture, particularly raising cattle, has long been important to the area's finances. The U.S. government located an agricultural research station in Woodward in 1912, and Oklahoma's first commercial-grade cattle auction opened here in 1933. Although the end of the open range brought a temporary emphasis to row crop farming, beginning with corn, broomcorn and cotton, later followed by wheat, the cattle industry soon rebounded, particularly after introduction of the Hereford breed in the early twentieth century.

Riffel praised the progressive attitude of Woodward's citizens, noting that three separate tax initiatives totaling approximately $40 million have recently been approved by large margins, although each involved increased taxes.

"Among these are recreational and quality-of-life projects including renovation of a 160 acre park complex, construction of a Conference Center, upgrades to an eighteen hole golf course, a water park, ball fields and other facilities," he said.

Right: Marquee at the Arts.
PHOTOGRAPH COURTESY OF MIKE KLEMME.

Below: Fuller Ballpark.
PHOTOGRAPH COURTESY OF MIKE KLEMME.

Citizen-approved bond projects also included revitalization of Woodward's Main Street, which included the Streetscape Project (lighting, streets and sidewalk improvements.)

Recent business, commercial and education facilities have also been added, along with new residences. Although Woodward had been without a movie theater for years, it now has a six-screen cineplex.

Enrollment and curriculum at the Woodward Campus of Northwest Oklahoma State University have increased steadily since opening of the facilities several years ago. This campus offers a permanent site at which area residents can receive a quality education near home.

With a population of about 15,000, Woodward is the largest city in an area of nine counties, and is a northwest Oklahoma commercial hub for a tri-state region with over 70,000 residents. The U.S. Census Bureau has listed Woodward as the second fastest-growing community in Oklahoma, with a 2010-2013 population increase of 6.6 percent.

Woodward's recently adopted comprehensive plan for the next twenty years includes tools and resources to enhance a robust community embracing regionalism, fiscal responsibility and a strong quality of life. This plan is designed to enhance the city as a northwest Oklahoma commercial hub in an attractive setting while embracing family values and a rich cultural heritage.

Above: The Conference Center.
PHOTOGRAPH COURTESY OF MIKE KLEMME.

Below: Geese and train at Crystal Beach.
PHOTOGRAPH COURTESY OF MIKE KLEMME.

CITY OF PRAGUE

Above: Prague City Park and gazebo.

Below: Saint Wenceslaus Catholic Church and the National Shrine of the Infant Jesus of Prague.

With a 9.7 percent population growth from 2000-2010, the City of Prague continues to build on more than a century of history toward continued development for the future. Founded on November 28, 1902, Prague is known as a "Small Town with a Big Heart."

When the Sac and Fox Indian Reservation land in Southeast Oklahoma opened for settlement in the 1891 Land Run, its participants included unrelated groups of Bohemians and Germans who had come to North America to escape political tyranny in their native countries.

They settled near where the Fort Smith and Western Railroad would locate its coal chute and train station in 1902, leading to the platting of a new town. Eva Barta and other settlers named the town "Praha," which was Anglicized to "Prague."

The earliest post office was called Barta, with the name changed after a few months to Prague, Oklahoma Territory. By July 24, 1902, Prague had 2 banks, 2 hotels, 5 restaurants, 2 barbershops, 6 saloons, a drugstore, furniture store, 2 hardware stores, 2 meat markets, 2 lumberyards, a blacksmith shop, 3 doctors, and 6 general merchandise stores. Materials and stock had to be transported by wagon

from the nearest railroad, which was twenty-five miles away. Residents utilized the rich land for farming, with cotton as the most important cash crop for some years. Relatively high cotton prices led others to sell their crops in Prague, and 10,000 bales were marketed here in 1904, leading to a local boom.

Located only three miles from Indian Territory, where prohibition was enforced, both whites and Indians obtained their alcoholic refreshments in Prague, which soon had thirteen saloons, leading to law enforcement problems during the next five years. Liquor was shipped from the little town at the bottom of trunks purchased from local merchants. Tightly packed dry goods covered bottles of whiskey on the trunks' bottoms for shipment to Indian Territory. After Oklahoma was admitted to the Union in 1907, prohibition was enforced and the Prague saloons closed.

A commission plan of city government was adopted in 1902 with B. F. Whitmore as the first mayor. In 1927 this was replaced by a mayor-council type of government. A $47,000 bond election financed construction of water and electrical systems built in 1909, and in 1925, another $30,000 in bonds provided sewage disposal. Two years later the city built its first white way lighting system and natural gas lines.

Prague's earliest students attended school in a small wood building. When it became overcrowded, classes were taught in Bohemian Hall, O. T. Garage and elsewhere. A four room brick school was built in 1904, with a second story added later. The high school was established in 1905 and accredited in 1908. With a current enrollment topping 1,000 students, more recent additions to Prague's school system have included a new high school

completed in 1960, followed by a gymnasium, community center, and other buildings; two elementary schools and a media center. One of the elementary schools was above ground and the other was underground, for protection from tornadoes. The district acquired and remodeled a shopping center to house its middle school classrooms and an auditorium.

Prague citizens are served by a twenty-five bed hospital and clinic with offices for medical personnel, as well as a modern seventy-eight bed nursing home. A 300 acre city-owned lake provides fishing and recreation facilities. Prague also has a nine-hole golf course, tennis courts, a swimming pool and rodeo grounds, as well as baseball, softball and football fields. A good airport with a 3,600 foot lighted runway provides not only an office and hangers, but fuel as well. The Haynie Public Library provides books, E-books, DVDs and computer access for preschoolers through senior citizens, as well as a meeting room with video conferencing equipment.

The Prague Historical Museum on Jim Thorpe Boulevard includes a monument to Jim Thorpe, the outstanding twentieth century athlete and Olympic gold medal winner. Thorpe was born on a farm south of Prague. The museum also recognizes Olinka Hrdy, a noted artist born in Indian Territory near Prague in 1902. Hrdy's work has been treasured worldwide. The National Shrine of the Infant Jesus of Prague, which is located in Saint Wenceslaus Catholic Church, attracts over 60,000 visitors to the city each year. St. Wenceslaus is one of the city's fifteen churches, which include several that were recently built, remodeled or enlarged.

Because of its Czech heritage, Prague chose "The Kolache Festival" to celebrate the anniversary of its founding. The first such festival was held in 1951, followed the next year by the city's "Golden Anniversary" celebration. Thousands of visitors from throughout the world now attend this annual event, which features a parade, street dancing, entertainment and good food.

Although still primarily a farming/ranching community, Prague is moving toward industry and commerce, with manufacturing adding to its diversification. With an ideal location between two interstate highways, a forty acre industrial park is being developed for future growth. As with most of Oklahoma, oil and gas production still provide the foundation of this segment of the economy.

Above: Prague streetscape looking north on Highway 99.

Below: Prague Historical Museum and Jim Thorpe Monument.

CITY OF ELK CITY

For over a century, Elk City, Oklahoma residents have patiently explained that their town has always been named for nearby Elk Creek. Signatures on Elk City's 1901 plat included V. O. Boone, surveyor; Beeks Erick, Choctaw Townsite and Development Co. president; H. E. Bonebrake, the company's secretary; and Charles H. Dwaide, manager. Election ballots approved Elk City's incorporation as a village that year. When Oklahoma became a state and county lines were redrawn, Elk City was shown on the map of Beckham County. These facts are used to combat a persistent myth that the town was originally named Busch, a misconception apparently stemming from post office names. In 1901, because an Elk Post Office already existed in Oklahoma Territory, the Postmaster General nixed a request for one named Elk City. Instead, he approved an alternate request to name the post office Busch. When Elk became Pooleville in 1907, Elk City residents finally obtained mail service under their town's proper name.

Elk City's location was chosen because five Weatherford men knew the Choctaw, Oklahoma & Gulf Railroad was scheduled to be built through there. They purchased 320 acres on the railroad's route. In 1904, after regular train service had begun, Rock Island bought the line.

Early development of Elk City included an eight-grade school taught in tents by Professor J. E. Delaney, principal, Professor J. B. Conley and Miss Lizzie Caudill in 1901, prior to construction of a building. Twelve grades were offered by 1904. Elk City's earliest churches were the Methodist Episcopal North and an established Baptist Church relocated—building and all—from Old Canute. The Baptists shared their building with the Methodists and Presbyterians until those churches could be built. Other early denominations were Methodist Episcopal South, Church of Christ, Catholic, Christian, United Brethren, and Seventh Day Adventist. The Elk City Commercial Club, forerunner of the chamber of commerce, was organized in 1902, with twenty-nine charter members.

Dr. Tom E. Standifer built Elk City's first hospital, Florence Sanitarium. The Thurmonds— A. L.; E. K.; I. C.; and O. H., along with A. L. Taylor—were directors of First National Bank, which was authorized nine days after sale of the city's first lots. Still operating under the same family leadership, this is the city's oldest business. Others began soon afterward, including blacksmiths, grocers, a brick manufacturer, distiller, dry goods and hardware stores, livery and stable, saloon and hotel, grist mill, lumber yards, wagon yards, two newspapers, electric company/cotton gin, and mill cooperative.

In 1912 local Presbyterian ladies started what later became a Carnegie Library in 1915. That decade also brought new hospitals, construction of U.S. 66 through Elk City, a Dr. Pepper Bottling Co. that has been recognized for the largest production per capita in the world, and what is now the Beutler & Son Rodeo Co. The latter is a four-generation family operation that has produced rodeos across the U.S. for over eighty years.

The 1930s saw the opening of Community Hospital, the country's first cooperative hospital. Its founder, Dr. Michael Shadid, began the concept of pre-paid group medical care. Other highlights included appointment of Mattie Ellen Thompson as Oklahoma's first woman police chief; establishment of the Kelly Creamery, which processed and packaged dairy products distributed in four states; purchase of *The Elk City Daily News*, now in the third generation of Wade family operation; and the opening of Ackley Park.

Shell Oil Co. drilled the first well in a vast oil field in the Elk City area in 1946, followed by other drilling companies. In the next decade, over 700 wells were completed in the area. Shell built a large gasoline extraction plant south of Elk City in the early 1950s, and "oil money" hugely impacted the area's economy. Reactivation of the military base at nearby Burns Flat brought in numerous military personnel and a boom in civilian jobs. The oil field, air force base, and good agricultural years led to a strong local economy. Elk City's semi-pro baseball team, the Elks, had legendary success in this era, winning league championship 1948-51 and many additional titles. Several players went on to distinguished pro-baseball careers.

Highlights of the 1960s included continued school reorganization that started in 1955, and establishment of Old Town Museum, followed in the 1970s by airport improvements and flood control efforts. Natural gas explorations and drilling in the Andarko Basin led to the second boom, which lasted until 1982, when the national economy tanked.

More recent highlights have included crowning of Susan Powell, an Elk City native, as Miss America in 1981; election of Teresa Mullican to eight terms as mayor; a dramatic increase in drilling after the 9/11 attack, escalating a third boom; a change of Elk City's economic emphasis from agriculture to oil and gas; establishment of the city's status as a regional retail and medical center, including opening of the Great Plains Regional Medical Center's new hospital; approval of the city's own ambulance service, operated through the fire department; and construction of the new city hall on Centennial Square.

Population statistics for Elk City show growth from 3,165 in 1910 to 12,606 estimated for 2013.

CITY OF CHANDLER

Since it was first opened for settlement in a "Land Run" on September 28, 1891, people have been "Choosing Chandler" as a unique place to live, work, and visit. Chandler's birth began with a bang when gunshots were fired at high noon to signal the land opening. Thousands of settlers, both men and women, ran to stake their claim on one of the 2,208 free lots that had been plotted in the 320 acre town site. The site was located on a hill overlooking Indian Springs, a main source of water at the time, and the lowlands, which now include the city's main gathering spot, Tilghman Park, and Bell Cow Creek.

Today, nearly 6,500 people who live inside and outside the city call Chandler home. They enjoy the small town charm and big city convenience that Chandler offers by being nestled in the rolling sand rock hills on historic Route 66 between Oklahoma City and Tulsa. Chandler area residents also have access to good schools, numerous sports venues for its youth, numerous retail establishments including a vibrant main street, an array of churches, an active Senior Citizens' Center, a stable local economy supported by well-established businesses, along with recreational opportunities for both young and old.

Prior to its founding, Chandler had already been chosen to be the county seat of Lincoln County because of its central location.

More than 100 years later, it was fitting that Chandler entered the twenty-first century as a center of attention for retail trade in Central Oklahoma with a diversified economic base that included insurance, manufacturing and processing, construction, transportation, agriculture and energy.

Over time, the City of Chandler in area has increased ten-fold to keep pace with growing public needs, to improve the quality of life for its residents, and to become a destination point for tourists. The city's 3,200 acres encompasses the Bell Cow Lake water supply and recreation area, parks and walking trails, popular equestrian trails, a swimming pool, a nine-hole public golf course back-dropped by Chandler Lake, and a regional airport. Other attractions include the Route 66 Interpretive Center, the Lincoln County Museum of Pioneer History, and the nearby Ioway Casino operated by the Ioway Indian Tribe. Also, Chandler is especially proud to be the home of the 160th Field Artillery Battalion of the Oklahoma National Guard.

As the Chandler community has grown, its leaders and public officials have remained committed to "the basics"—addressing infrastructure needs and keeping citizens safe. The people of Chandler look to the future while remembering their past.

For more information on the City of Chandler, visit www.chandlerok.com.

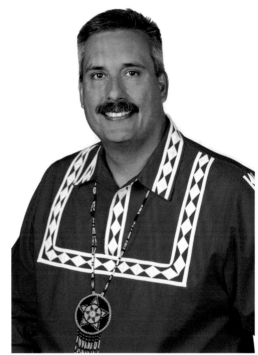

CHOCTAW NATION OF OKLAHOMA

The Choctaw are native to the Southeastern United States and members of the Muskogean linguistic family, which traces its roots to a mound-building, maize-based society that flourished in the Mississippi River Valley for more than 1,000 years before European contact.

Although their first encounter with Europeans ended in a bloody battle with Hernando de Soto's fortune-hunting expedition in 1540, the Choctaw would come to embrace European traders who arrived in their homeland nearly two centuries later. The Choctaw became known as one of America's Five Civilized Tribes, which also includes the Chickasaw, Cherokee, Seminole and Creek.

The Choctaw signed nine treaties with the United States before the Civil War, beginning with the Treaty of Hopewell in 1786, which set boundaries and established universal peace between the two nations. Subsequent treaties, however, reshaped those borders and forced the Choctaw to cede millions of acres of land. In 1830 the United States seized the last of the Choctaw's ancestral territory and relocated the Tribe to Indian Territory west of the Mississippi. The Choctaw were the first to walk the Trail of Tears. Nearly 2,500 members perished along the way. Despite the many lives lost, the Choctaw remained a hopeful and generous people. The first order of business upon arriving in their new homeland was to start a school and a church. They drafted a new constitution.

Today, the Choctaw Nation of Oklahoma is the third largest Tribe in the world with over 200,000 members. Its service area is comprised of ten and a half counties in southeastern Oklahoma, divided into twelve districts, and leaders are continuously working to make sure there is hope for our future. As federal services for our children are reduced, the Choctaw Nation is securing funding and developing specific programs to ensure the next generations have hope and pride to carry on.

Many of the services and programs of the Tribe, such as the Head Starts, education scholarships, career development, health clinics and job placement opportunities, go a long way toward helping Tribal members meet this vision. Such programs include academic recognition, higher education assistance, career development, emergency assistance, loan programs for housing, and veteran' advocacy. The Tribe has been extremely blessed to be successful in businesses such as gaming, travel plazas and manufacturing. These business profits pay for services that can be offered to Tribal people all over the world. Federal dollars assist in many programs, but without the business revenues, there would be many individuals left without help.

Left: Chief Gary Batton.

Right: Assistant Chief Jack Austin, Jr.

CHICKASAW NATION

Above: Bill Anoatubby, governor of the Chickasaw Nation.

Since Bill Anoatubby was elected governor of the Chickasaw Nation in 1987, the tribe has become a major force in a positive transformation underway in southern Oklahoma. In recent years that transforming power has had an increasingly powerful effect on the entire state.

Most have heard the phrase "a rising tide lifts all boats." While that metaphor has been used effectively to illustrate the idea that a growing economy benefits everyone, it could be extended to just as effectively illustrate the same principle with any indicator of the quality of life.

A growing economy benefits everyone concerned because more money circulating in the economy means rewarding employment is more readily available, people are more likely to have access to disposable income and new businesses are more likely to succeed.

There is a similar dynamic at work in regard to other factors affecting the quality of life.

Better hospitals, staffed with more doctors, nurses and other healthcare providers, naturally lead to easier access to quality healthcare.

More highly qualified, motivated law enforcement officers equipped with first-rate tools of the trade improves public safety.

While a rising tide begins with a robust, growing economy, that tide truly lifts all boats when the money produced is reinvested into the community, leading to more business opportunities, pride in community, higher quality healthcare, a more effective transportation system and more confidence in the level of public safety.

That is the reason the Chickasaw Nation, under the visionary leadership of Governor Anoatubby, takes a comprehensive view of a variety of factors as it strives to achieve its mission to enhance the overall quality of life of the Chickasaw people.

A healthy, growing economy is the foundation of that mission and the tribe has focused a great deal of time and energy on economic development.

Since the Chickasaw Nation began operating its first tribal business in 1972, the tribe has made a concerted effort to build a sustainable source of revenue by diversifying its business portfolio.

When the Chickasaw Nation opened its first business, the Chickasaw Motor Inn in Sulphur, Oklahoma, it developed a wide range of other opportunities and now operates more than 100 successful businesses.

Less than three decades ago, in 1987, the Chickasaw Nation operated just over thirty programs with more than ninety percent of the funding coming from the federal government. The budget for federal programs was little more than $7 million.

Today, successful tribal economic development efforts enable the Chickasaw Nation to fund a majority of its programs and services. The tribe offers more than 200 tribally funded programs. The tribal budget has grown exponentially, funding services from education, healthcare and nutrition to housing and family services.

Although the primary goals of economic development are providing revenue for the tribe's government and funding for programs and services, there is ample evidence the Chickasaw Nation is making a significant contribution to the overall health of the economy in Oklahoma.

A study found that the Chickasaw Nation had an economic impact of more than $2.4 billion on the Oklahoma economy in 2011 and supported approximately 16,000 jobs in Oklahoma.

Chickasaw Nation businesses generated $1.39 billion from tribal business activities, which include manufacturing, banking, tourism, energy, healthcare, hospitality and entertainment.

At the time of the study, the Chickasaw Nation employed more than 10,000 people in Oklahoma with $318 million in direct payroll contributions. That makes the tribe the seventh largest employer in Oklahoma, surpassing even the U.S. Postal Service.

Multiplier effects of Chickasaw Nation operations helped create more than 5,900 additional jobs with a payroll of more than $206 million. In total, tribal business and governmental operations resulted in $525 million in income for Oklahoma workers.

While this contribution to the health of the Oklahoma economy is meaningful in itself, it is made even more significant

because the revenues of tribal businesses are reinvested in ways that enhance business opportunities across the state and support the health and well-being of Chickasaws and other Oklahomans.

As part of efforts to diversify its business operations, the Chickasaw Nation is in the midst of an initiative to develop tourism facilities. Much of the impact of that initiative can be seen in Sulphur, Davis, and other parts of Murray County.

A core part of that initiative is the Chickasaw Cultural Center near Sulphur. Since it opened in July 2010 more than 300,000 visitors from around the world have flocked to the cultural center to experience Chickasaw history and culture.

Other new venues in Murray County include the Artesian Hotel, Bedré Fine Chocolate factory, ARTesian art gallery, Chickasaw Travel Stop, Chickasaw Welcome Center, Chickasaw Visitor Center, as well as the Chickasaw Retreat and Conference Center.

"Tourism has long been a major part of the Oklahoma economy and we believe these new facilities could play a significant role in Murray County's efforts to increase tourism in this part of the state," said Governor Anoatubby. "The original Artesian Hotel was the centerpiece of the community for decades and it is easy to see how this new hotel could complement all the wonderful tourism opportunities this area has to offer."

These new facilities are part of the larger tourism initiative the tribe is undertaking throughout the state. Other efforts to increase tourism in Oklahoma include expansion of casinos, renovation of Remington Park, the restoration of the Chickasaw Capitol in Tishomingo and the White House in Emet as well as restoration of the historic McSwain Theatre in Ada.

As one of the largest industries in Oklahoma, tourism impacts businesses from hotels to restaurants, convenience stores, retail businesses, antique shops and farmers' markets, to name a few.

"We believe this investment will benefit the economy far into the future, because tourism has a significant ripple effect," said Governor Anoatubby. "Beyond the economic impact, we believe these new facilities will help enhance the sense of pride that comes along with being an Oklahoman."

Access to quality healthcare is another area where the Chickasaw Nation is making a major contribution to the quality of life of all Oklahomans.

In 1987 the Indian Health Service operated Carl Albert Indian Health Facility in Ada, along with two health clinics, one in Tishomingo and one in Ardmore.

Today, the tribe compacts with the federal government to operate the entire health system, which was formerly administered by the Indian Health Service. One of the most visible signs of that contribution is the Chickasaw Nation Medical Center, which opened in July 2010. At 370,000 square feet, the state-of-the-art healthcare facility is almost triple the size of the

Top, left: bedré Café.

Top, right: The bedré Fine Chocolate Factory interior.

Above: The bedré Fine Chocolate Factory exterior.

Below: The Artesian Hotel.

Chickasaw Nation Medical Center.

Carl Albert Indian Health Facility it replaced. Features include a seventy-two bed hospital, level 3 emergency department, ambulatory care facility, diabetes care center, dental clinic, diagnostic imaging center, women's health center, tribal health programs as well as a centrally located "town center" bridging the centers of patient care.

Since the facility was opened, the Chickasaw Nation has also opened new healthcare clinics in Ardmore and Tishomingo.

The 66,000 square foot clinic in Ardmore is six times larger than the original building. New and expanded services include behavioral health, physical therapy, drive-thru pharmacy, audiology, ultrasound, dexa scan and mammography. Additionally, staff has increased from twenty-five to approximately 100 employees.

At 53,000 square feet, the clinic in Tishomingo is more than four times larger than the clinic it replaced. Services available at the new clinic include dental, behavioral health, drive-thru pharmacy, ultrasound exams, mammograms, bone density scans and hearing exams.

"Our healthcare team works diligently to offer the high-quality healthcare so vital to the overall quality of life," said Governor Anoatubby. "These new clinics are designed and equipped to empower our staff with the best tools available."

These new facilities are part of the Chickasaw Nation Department of Health, which served more than 514,000 patient visits and filled more than 1.2 million prescriptions in FY 2013. That equals a daily average of 1,400 patient visits and more than 3,200 prescriptions.

Since Chickasaws and other Native Americans who receive healthcare services offered through the Chickasaw Nation Department of Health are part of the larger healthcare service population, these

services improve access to healthcare for all Oklahomans.

Beyond that, the experience and knowledge the Chickasaw Nation has gained through the operation of its tribal healthcare system has led the tribe to develop a private healthcare business, which offers healthcare to employees and other Oklahomans who are not citizens of a Native American nation.

In 2011, Sovereign Medical Solutions, an economic enterprise of the Chickasaw Nation, opened its first private practice family clinic and pharmacy in Ada. In 2014 the tribe opened its second such facility in Norman.

"This new business enables us to leverage the knowledge we have gained through the operation of our tribal healthcare system to develop healthcare services, which will help meet the needs of employees and other area residents," said Governor Anoatubby. "Adding another choice for high quality healthcare enhances the quality of life of everyone in the area. This clinic also helps add to economic development potential by offering vital services and additional opportunities for meaningful employment."

As part of its commitment to serve Chickasaws and other Oklahomans, the Chickasaw Nation reestablished the Lighthorse Police Department (LPD). Reestablished in 2004, the LPD has rapidly grown into an effective agency dedicated to protecting and serving all Oklahomans.

One overarching goal of the department is to overcome jurisdictional issues created by the patchwork of Indian land in Oklahoma that sometimes hinders law enforcement efforts.

Many of these jurisdictional issues were highlighted in a report by Amnesty International titled "Maze of Injustice: The failure to protect Indigenous women from sexual violence in the USA."

The report noted that "complicated jurisdictional issues can significantly delay

and prolong the process of investigating and prosecuting crimes of sexual violence."

In order to address the issue, a uniform cross-deputation agreement was created and signed by state and tribal leaders in 2005. This agreement provides a framework to enable all law enforcement officers in the state to make lawful arrests inside and outside Indian Country within the state of Oklahoma.

While the agreement applies to all law enforcement agencies in the state, special law enforcement commissions must be issued before law enforcement officers are authorized to take action in the jurisdiction of another agency.

In 2007 the Lighthorse made history by signing the first cross-deputation agreement with the Oklahoma Bureau of Narcotics and Dangerous Drugs. This agreement was the first of its kind between an American Indian police department and a state law enforcement agency.

"This agreement marks a major milestone in tribal-state relations, which will benefit every citizen in the state," said Governor Anoatubby at the time. "Combining the talents of these fine officers and other resources of these agencies will multiply the effectiveness of their efforts."

Since that time, the LPD has signed several special law enforcement commissions with numerous other state and local agencies. This enables the LPD to share its resources, including K-9 units, narcotics investigators, Special Weapons and Tactics team, and dive team with other agencies.

"Police protection is one of the most vital services any government offers its citizens," said Governor Anoatubby. "Therefore, we want to ensure our Lighthorse officers are highly-trained and well-equipped to work with other agencies to meet their responsibility to all Oklahomans."

Just as the Chickasaw Nation works closely with state and local law enforcement agencies to enhance public safety, the tribe also works closely with state and local governments to improve the safety and drivability of Oklahoma roads.

Each year, the Chickasaw Nation invests approximately $8 million in road maintenance and construction projects within its jurisdictional boundaries in south central Oklahoma.

One example is a project at the intersection of Main Street and Latta Road in Ada. The Chickasaw Nation worked closely with the City of Ada on that project to ease traffic congestion and enhance safety at the intersection.

The project involved installing traffic lights, constructing new turn lanes, installing additional streetlights and paving a sidewalk to transform what has been called one of the most dangerous intersections in Pontotoc County into one of the safest.

Whether it involves economic development, healthcare, public safety, transportation or the numerous other services offered by the Chickasaw Nation to enhance the quality of life of the Chickasaw people, they all have one thing in common.

Each of the programs and services which are part of the rising tide known as the Chickasaw Nation reach far beyond the Chickasaw people to lift all Oklahomans to greater heights.

"We are experiencing a true renaissance in almost all aspects of our tribe," said Governor Anoatubby. "Whether it is on the level of an individual citizen, or the tribe as a whole, we have made significant progress in education, government, the economy, healthcare and social welfare.

"We are dedicated to working together to strengthen our nation and being good neighbors to all. As leaders of the tribe strive to accomplish our primary mission 'to enhance the overall quality of life of Chickasaw citizens' it gives us great pleasure to know that our efforts have the ripple effect of enhancing the quality of life of all Oklahomans."

The Chickasaw Nation Health Clinic in Armore.

THE QUAPAW

This page and opposite: These historic mining photographs were taken in early day Ottawa County, Oklahoma, in Quapaw Territory, and signify the important role the area played in its history.

The Quapaw, also known as "Ug'Akhpa" or "Downstream People" in their language, settled hundreds of years ago in the area now known as Arkansas. In prehistoric times, the Tribe belonged to the southern part of the Siouan linguistic family, which migrated and relocated near the James and Savannah River region on the Atlantic Coast. Later, the group travelled back west and down the Ohio River to the mouth of the Mississippi River where they divided. One band travelled downstream and into present day Arkansas, and the other band travelled north settling on the Missouri River in present day Nebraska, where they later become known as the Omaha, or "Upstream People."

When French explorers arrived in 1673, there were approximately 10,000 Quapaw Indians living in four villages near the mouth of the Arkansas River. They referred to the Quapaw as "Arkansea," from which the river and the state became known as "Arkansas." By 1780 the Tribe had migrated further up the Arkansas River near the mouth of the White River. Early records described the Quapaw as peaceful people living in villages elevated on mounds of earth. The houses, containing several families, were long and covered with bark. They were agricultural people raising corn, squash, beans, pumpkins and gourds. They also gathered nuts, seeds and roots.

The men hunted deer, buffalo, bear, and wild turkey and caught fish out of the rivers.

Unfortunately, after the Louisiana Purchase in 1803, and later the organization of the Arkansas Territory, the Quapaw were forced to cede their land to the United States. In 1824 the Quapaw were removed to live in the area of the Caddo, near the Red River in Louisiana. Because of flooding, the new land was uninhabitable and they were forced to return to their original lands. By 1839 a reservation had been established in Northeastern Oklahoma. However, by then, the tribal number had been diminished to less than 100 enrolled members. More recently the number of enrolled Quapaw numbered around 2,000 (today about 4,000), with most of the members living near Miami, Oklahoma. There are no remaining pure blood Quapaw alive today. The last full-blood Quapaw on record, Robert Whitebird, died in 2005, at the age of ninety-two.

With the recognition of tribal sovereignty in the nineteenth century, the Quapaw Tribe began government relations with the United States with the treaty signed in 1818. The Tribe has continued relations through six subsequent treaties and agreements with the United States including the Quapaw Allotment Act of 1895, and continuing thereafter. The Quapaw Tribe has been governed pursuant to the "Resolution Delegating Authority to the Quapaw Tribal Business Committee to Speak and Act on Behalf of the Quapaw Tribe of Indians," as approved by the General Council of the Tribe on August 19, 1956.

Today, the Tribe's number has grown substantially, and their remaining territory is a 526 acre area in the extreme northeast corner of Oklahoma near the border of Missouri and Kansas. The Tribe's museum and library is now housed in the Robert Whitebird Quapaw Center in Quapaw, Oklahoma. Historical pictures and family information line the museum walls and include names such as Leading Fox and

Crawfish. Historic photographs and artifacts are also on display in the lobby of the Downstream Casino, which opened in July 2008.

The Downstream Casino is Northeast Oklahoma's only Las Vegas style destination resort and is located on the historic Tri-State corner where the Oklahoma, Missouri and Kansas state lines intersect, just off I-44. The resort is owned and operated by the Downstream Development Authority on behalf of the Quapaw Tribe. After opening on July 5, 2008, the resort has added an additional $60 million in development expansion. The casino features a 75,000 square foot gaming floor with a state-of-the-art ventilation/air filtration system, thereby providing a virtually smoke-free environment. There are 2,000 electronic gaming machines, 36 live table games, and a 14 table, state-of-the-art Poker Room. The lobby includes a large metal sculpture in the shape of a pottery vessel, historical tribal photographs, and a bronze laser reproduction of artist Charles Banks Wilson's artwork entitled, *Quapaw Man*. Wilson married a Quapaw woman, and painted several portraits of the last pureblood men and women of the Tribe.

The property also includes a hotel with a 12 story tower featuring 222 upscale rooms, 15 luxury one and two-bedroom units, and a penthouse level VIP lounge. There is an outdoor pool with bar, cabanas, hot tub, and a twenty-four hour fitness center. Another tower with 152 upscale rooms offers the Nee Spa with five treatments rooms, salon, sauna, steam rooms and whirlpools. Other upscale amenities include valet parking and Wi-Fi connection.

Fine dining is available at the Red Oak Steakhouse featuring steaks and seafood, and the Spring River Buffet features an upscale international buffet with display cooking

stations. The Buffalo Grille offers casual dining and serves breakfast, lunch and dinner, and the "Wa-Na-Bee-Dea," meaning "come eat" in the Quapaw language, is a twenty-four hour food court and snack bar. Also onsite is the "Ma-Ko-Sha" coffee shop and bakery, Legends Sports Bar, Lover's Leap hotel lobby bar and lounge, and Devils Promenade, an upscale bar and lounge at the center of the casino floor.

Conference and meeting facilities include the Downstream Pavilion with a 1,000 person capacity multipurpose events center. Six banquet rooms are available with a total capacity of 400 people. For entertainment, the Legends Sports Bar Stage hosts live music on weekends and The Venue at Downstream offers an outdoor concert facility with a capacity of 6,000 people. For those interested in playing a round of golf, the Eagle Creek Golf Club offers a pristine 18-hole championship course with club house and restaurant. Special stay and play packages are available with the Downstream Hotel & Spa.

As a convenience for customers and travelers alike, a state-of-the-art convenience store and gas station is available on a fourteen acre site on the Missouri side of the Downstream property. There is even a charging station for electric vehicles. Parking is available for twenty-two semi-tractor-trailer trucks and there is an RV Park with forty spaces providing full water and electricity hook-ups.

The Downstream Development Authority is governed by a five-member board, including the Chairman of the Tribe's Business Committee, John L. Berrey; Secretary and Treasurer of the

Business Committee Tamara Smiley; Secretary and Treasurer of the Business Committee, George R. McWatters, Jr.; Marilyn Rogers; and Larry Ramsey. The overall impact of Downstream Casino Resort has generated more than $225 million in economic output annually, creating more than 1,640 permanent jobs. Oklahoma, Missouri, and Kansas are all enhanced economically from revenue, taxes, and jobs created from the casino. The tribal impact is significant as Downstream distributes $10 million a year to the Quapaw Tribe earmarked toward tribal services such as healthcare, environmental service, senior centers, a children's learning center, scholarships, and subsidizing housing for Tribal members. With the opening of Downstream's new Kappa hotel tower, spa, and other amenities, the economic output is projected to reach about $300 million annually, as well as creating a total of 1,880 permanent jobs. In addition to the large casino, there is also the Quapaw Casino, several miles north of Miami, Oklahoma.

Much credit is given to the Tribe's chairman and leader, John Berrey, who has been responsible for the Tribe's success over the last fourteen years. Berrey has served the Tribe not only in the capacity of chairman, but as an active leader in Indian Country, serving as vice chairman and board member of the Inter-Tribal Monitoring Association, member of the Inter-Tribal Council of Ottawa County, Oklahoma, representative to the United States Department of the Interior's Trust Reform Initiatives, and board of directors of the Claremore Indian Hospital. He has also served as spokesman for the Tribe, and has testified numerous times before congressional committees and worked with various government representatives to promote Indian legislation. Berrey was also appointed to the Advisory Council for Historic Preservation by President Bush in September 2008.

The Quapaw Tribe has also received two national humanitarian awards for volunteer efforts, particularly with the Joplin, Missouri, tornado disaster in May 2011. The Joplin

tornado was declared the worst tornado in American history in terms of death and property damage. The Tribe responded with members who spent months assisting in tornado recovery and relief work, and offering over $400,000 in goods, services, and donations toward the recovery effort. Many employees were allowed to assist in the relief instead of going to work. Fifty-eight employees of the casino lost their homes during the Joplin tornado; some lost family members to the disaster. The City of Joplin is the closet major community, where many employees live. The Tribe's response to this disaster and tragedy highlights their commitment to community.

In addition to the humanitarian awards, Downstream Casino Resort was awarded Tribal Enterprise of the Year, 2012, by the National Center for American Indian Enterprise Development. Downstream also participates in and sponsors numerous community service partnerships, and gives more than $500,000 each year to community and charitable organizations in all four states— Oklahoma, Missouri, Kansas, and Arkansas. The overall mission of the casino is to improve the lives of not only tribal members, but all communities and citizens in the entire Tri-State Region, as well as their home in Arkansas.

The Quapaw's long history of losing their land, and the struggles that followed, to their successful return to their homelands in Arkansas, has come full circle. The Quapaw story is that of a friendly, generous people, who have survived, and the financial success of the Downstream Casino reflects the Tribe's continued survival and return to prominence. Additionally, the Tribe has secured the resources to prosper and take care of their community, and preserve their cultural heritage.

For more information on the Quapaw Tribe, and Downstream Casino Resort, go to www.quapawtribe.com and www.downstream-casino.com.

Above: The exquisite lobby of the Downstream Casino Resort Hotel.

Below: A night time view of the beautiful Downstream Casino Resort.

WYANDOTTE NATION

Prior to European contact more than a dozen tribes along the St. Lawrence River and Upper Great Lakes Region collectively called themselves Wendat. They were all closely related with many cultural similarities, yet they each retained unique tribal names. Five of those tribes comprised a powerful confederacy known as the Wendat (Huron) Confederacy. The founders of the confederacy were the Attignawantan. Another tribe, the Tionontati, lived adjacent to the Attignawantan; however, they were not part of the Wendat Confederacy. After a series of wars and ensuing defeat at the hands of the Iroquois Confederacy, in the early 1650s these people joined two other dispersed people groups—the Wenrohronon, and Attawandaron. They henceforth united as one, set aside their unique tribal names, and collectively called themselves Wandat. The new tribal name was a unique dialectal variation of Wendat.

After being dispersed from their ancestral homelands, the Wandats settled near Fort Detroit in 1701. Within a few years a portion of the tribe ventured south into the Ohio Country. They eventually settled near what would become Upper Sandusky, Ohio. In Michigan and Ohio, after sustained contact with the British, their traditional name Wandat became corrupted and spelled as Wyandot. Pressure from settlers forced the Treaty of 1843 and their removal to land west of the Mississippi River (Kansas). Another Treaty in 1855 effactually terminated the Wyandot as a recognized tribe; however, in

1857, some Wyandots who were unwilling to accept United States citizenship relocated to Indian Territory (Oklahoma). After the Civil War concluded, the Treaty of 1867 reinstated the Wyandots as a tribe. By 1871 approximately 200 citizens had successfully reorganized a tribal government. The name Wyandotte was officially used after the 1867 Treaty and reflects an influence in its spelling from the French language. In 1937 the Wyandottes again reorganized under provisions of the Oklahoma Indian Welfare Act of 1936 and adopted the name—Wyandotte Tribe of Oklahoma. Upon adopting a new tribal constitution in 1999, Article I of the constitution again changed the tribal name to the Wyandotte Nation.

Today, the Wyandotte Nation claims over five thousand enrolled members nationwide with descendants still living in Oklahoma, Ohio, and the Canadian province of Ontario. Other estimates include approximately ten thousand Wyandotte descendants living primarily in the Great Lakes region of Canada and the United States. The tribe hosts their annual cultural days, including language and history classes, along with their Pow Wow and various cultural activities in September of each year.

Right: Bronze sculpture of a Wyandot Indian family, a tribute to the city's founding people, the Wyandots.

For the Wyandotte Nation, 2013 brought about many special events and achievements including the startup of a Tribal Court System enabling them to meet the requirements of their tribal constitution and further govern their own jurisdictions. Other highlights for 2013 included the first ever Tribal Town Hall Meetings held in Seattle, Washington, and Irvine and Sacramento, California, in an effort to connect tribal citizens. Future Tribal Town Hall meetings are planned in Texas and Colorado. The goal of these meetings is to unite and share information with members about the past, present and future among Wyandotte citizens across the entire country.

The Tribe has also opened the Wyandotte Nation Casino in Wyandotte, Oklahoma. The casino features a variety of game tables including 6 deck blackjack, 3 card poker, and single deck Superfun 21, and special tournaments are offered periodically. Also offered are slot machines featuring 532 class two and class three games with denominations ranging from .01 to $10. The Club Wyandotte offers special card rewards to its members. With Premier Rewards, players can enjoy benefits of using their points for a variety of purchases including merchandise, gas, food and other services. The casino also features fine dining and has plans to expand its services and entertainment to include a private club area, bowling alley, new Twin

Bridges Restaurant, VIP lounge, entertainment venue, and a billiards and darts room.

Further economic developments include the opening of the first Indian-owned Sonic restaurant in the United States in Seneca, Missouri. A fuel stop and convenience store is located just outside the community offering amenities for travelers. It also features a small casino called the Lucky Turtle Casino, as well as the Turtle Stop Diner. Other major revenue comes from the 7th Street Casino, which opened in Kansas City, Kansas, in September 2007. In addition, the Tribe runs and operates Wyandotte NeTel and Bearskin Services, which are suppliers of fiber optic information services to the U.S. Government. The tribe also operates Wyandotte Precision Products, which offers a strategic blend of machining, engineering, reverse engineering, manufacturing and machine build/rebuild capabilities, and a team of experienced machinists to solve many types of repair problems.

Other recent projects include a new community building in Heritage Acres that should be completed early in 2014. The community building will be a great asset for all tribal citizens living in the area. The Tribe is also planning for the groundbreaking of their new Tribal Cultural and Activity Center in 2014. The new activity center will provide a place and opportunity for the Tribe to share the history of the Wyandotte.

For more information about the Wyandotte Nation, please visit www.wyandotte-nation.org.

Above: Chief Billy Friend.

EASTERN SHAWNEE TRIBE OF OKLAHOMA

Top: The Social Services Building.

Above: Walter Bluejacket was elected the first chief of the Eastern Shawnee.

Below: Four Feathers Recycling Center.

Bottom: Community Center AOA Building.

Founded on December 22, 1939, the Eastern Shawnee Tribe provides benefits and services to its members and community including: library, print shop, cultural preservation, tribal police, children and family services, family violence prevention, meth and suicide prevention, tribal housing, wellness, environmental protection agency, administration on aging, and education. The Tribe also invests its energy in enterprises generating revenue for the benefit of tribal members with programs created through the ingenuity of tribal administrative departments and established successful ventures with business partners. Other businesses include Eastern Shawnee Tribal Enterprises, Native2Native HR Solutions, People's Bank of Seneca, Indigo Sky Casino, Whispering Woods RV Park, Outpost Casino, Eastern Shawnee Travel Center, Eastern Shawnee Print Shop, Four Feathers Recycling Center, and the George J. Captain Library.

Historically, the Eastern Shawnee Tribe of Oklahoma is one of three federally-recognized Shawnee Tribes—the Absentee Shawnee near Shawnee; the Eastern Shawnee in Ottawa County on the Oklahoma-Missouri border between the small towns of Wyandotte, Oklahoma, and Seneca, Missouri; and the Shawnee Tribe in Miami. These three tribes were unified as the Shawnee Nation and lived throughout the region east of the Mississippi River.

In 1830 the Indian Removal Act was passed and later declared illegal. It was followed by the 1831 Treaty with the Seneca, exchanging lands in Ohio for a reservation in Indian Territory in modern day Ottawa County, Oklahoma. In September 1832 the United States Military forced 258 Lewistown Shawnee and Seneca Indians to leave Ohio. Herded like cattle, they walked or rode on horseback for nearly 700 miles. Many died, leaving their bones, their names, their stories. Those who lived arrived in Indian Territory during a bitter cold December. They remained the Mixed Band until 1867 when the two groups separated and became known as the Seneca Cayuga and the Eastern Shawnee.

The formation of the Eastern Shawnee Tribe occurred sometime after May 21, 1937, and has since been led by many devoted leaders and visionary tribal members. Walter Bluejacket was elected the first chief of the Eastern Shawnee Tribe of Oklahoma in modern times. George F. (Buck) Captain was chief (1978-1996) when the Tribe constructed three new buildings on the original 58.19 acres, began gaming in 1984, and adopted a new constitution in 1994, which made the role of chief a fulltime position.

Buck was quite active. In 1984 a third building was constructed on 58.19 acres. The first two, an administrative building and an unfinished economic building, had been constructed during Chief James Greenfeather's term, which preceded Buck. The third building was the Nutrition Building (now known as the Sandy Captain Cultural Building). The empty and unfinished economic building opened on December 7, 1984, as the Eastern Shawnee Tribe of Oklahoma's Bingo operation, catapulting the Tribe into the gaming world. As a result of bingo profits, the Tribe made its first land purchase—112 acres on Highway 10C in 1986.

In 1990, Buck made an unprecedented move. Knowing that the three federally recognized Shawnee Tribes in

Oklahoma had not been together as a Nation for almost two hundred years, Buck contacted the Absentee Shawnee Tribe near Little Axe and the Loyal Shawnee Tribe, invited them to a dinner in the Nutrition Building and the rest is history.

In 1992 they saw the construction of the Bluejacket Center and the purchase of the Rickner property. In 1995 the Tribe made its first purchase of 1,750 shares in People's Bank of Seneca.

In his last year as chief, Buck oversaw the establishment of the George F. Captain Library, the Tribe becoming a Self-Governance Tribe, and the joint establishment of Bearskin Clinic, a health venture between the Wyandotte and Eastern Shawnee Tribes.

James (Jim) Greenfeather was chief (1974-1978) when he enlisted Robert Alexander to create the Eastern Shawnee Tribe Seal in 1975 to appear on the flag for the Bicentennial year 1976.

Charles Enyart was chief (1998-2006) when the Tribe amended the Constitution in 1999. He also oversaw the construction of the Housing Authority in 1998, Travel Plaza in 1999, Social Services in 2001, Bordertown Casino in 2003, and the Betty Jane Amundsen Museum in 2004. Glenna J. Wallace has been serving as chief since 2006. She has spearheaded numerous building projects and the development of infrastructure with roads, sewers, bridges, a water tower in 2007, and buildings such as Outpost Casino in 2008, Indian Child Welfare in 2009, Community Center/Agency on Aging and Wellness Center in 2010, People's Bank of Seneca in Loma Linda, Missouri, and Indigo Sky Casino in 2012, Public Safety and Woodland's Elder's Housing Complex in 2013.

While the income from Casinos and other Eastern Shawnee businesses helps provide essential services to its citizens, education remains among its core values. They award monetary incentives to high school students maintaining a strong grade point average and offer scholarship programs for college or vocational training.

Tribal Gaming for the Eastern Shawnee Tribe began in 1984 with Bingo and Pull Tabs in the in the Old Red Barn, now the Annex. The Outpost Casino was built in 2008 followed by the Indigo Sky Casino and Hotel in 2012.

Thanks to Indian Community Development Block Grant funds, four buildings of the Tribal Administration are now located on the Highway 10C Complex, with future plans to bring the entire Tribal Administration to this property. The property also includes the Eastern Shawnee Housing Authority, a Public Safety Building and "The Woodlands," an Elder Independent Living Complex.

In 2010 the Tribe constructed Four Feather Recycling in Seneca, Missouri. Due to the success of special events and partnering with both the Oklahoma Department of Environmental Quality and Keep America Beautiful Organization, the Tribe received an award from the Department of Environmental Quality in July of 2014.

To date the Tribe owns 2,390 acres and in 2015 will open Border Town Casino and Arena to the gaming public for more convention and meeting spaces, larger concerts and sporting events, and an arena. The Tribe is also anticipating an opening of a Child Learning Center in 2016.

Today, Tribal headquarters are located in the Bluejacket Building at 127 West Oneida in Wyandotte.

Above: The Bluejacket Administration Building.

Below: Glenna J. Wallace has been serving as chief since 2006.

Bottom: Indigo Sky Casino and Hotel.

MIAMI TRIBE OF OKLAHOMA

Right: Tribal Business Committee from left to right, Second Chief Dustin Olds, Secretary/Treasurer Sarah Lawson, Chief Douglas Lankford, Second Councilperson Scott Willard and First Councilperson Donya Williams.

Below: Tribal leader George Ironstrack leads Eewansaapita students in war cry during the annual Lacrosse match against Seneca Cayuga youth.

In our language we are Myaamia—the downstream people, now often pronounced Miami. The United States government recognizes us as a sovereign nation, the Miami Tribe of Oklahoma. We originate from the Great Lakes region, with homelands lying within Indiana, Ohio, Illinois, lower Michigan and Wisconsin.

We were exposed to early European contact through the Jesuit missions in the late 1600s, then the French and British invasion and the struggle for control of the region. In those days we numbered into tens of thousands.

During the years of struggle toward establishment of the United States of America, our people struggled to retain their homeland and connection to that landscape. Our stories, wisdom, victories and defeats are all recorded in history. We are known.

The Greenville Treaty of 1795 required the massive cession of lands, and vicious tenacity of this country's early leaders led to the Indian Removal Act of 1830, which altered our place and people forever.

Despite attempts to avoid our Tribe's removal beyond the Mississippi, required by the Treaty of 1840, our ancestors, numbering approximately 300 souls, were herded at gunpoint and forced onto boats to travel from eastern Indiana to the Ohio River. Steamboats then took them west, down the Ohio River to the Mississippi, up to the Missouri and across to Westport Landing near Kansas City. They

then traveled south by horseback and wagon to a reserve in the land of the Kaw people, near today's La Cygne, Kansas, where they remained until the Treaty of 1867 required them to move to the Indian Territory, known today as Oklahoma. Upon arrival here, our Nation numbered fewer than 100 adults.

Our first Tribal Constitution was adopted in 1939, officially recognizing us as the Miami Tribe of Oklahoma, and we have since been governed by elected leaders. This Tribal Business Committee continues the struggle to retain our sovereignty and demand our right to self-determination through our status as a self-governing Nation.

The Miami Tribe of Oklahoma has shown by action our absolute determination to perpetuate our cultural identity and to re-establish a land base for Myaamia citizens. Through our Cultural Resources Office, our Tribe has taken responsibility for the status of our resources.

In full knowledge of the devastating effects of the many assimilation tactics forced on our people over the past 150 years, it recognizes that our heritage, language and cultural knowledge will live on. It also supports reclamation, restoration, revitalization, preservation and perpetuation efforts in response to the effects of history and assimilation.

We actively reclaim what has been taken from us—our language, traditions, ancestral remains from museum shelves, and missing objects of our culture.

The Natural Resources Office works with the Nation's growing land-base, ensuring that Tribal land use is culturally appropriate. This includes assisting our people's return

to the landscape for cultural education and traditional activities, as well as using targeted areas for growing organic crops to support our people's health.

We restore our connection to each other and to the landscape through many annual gatherings on Tribal lands, and see our community's revitalization in the return of language and traditions. We preserve what has been reclaimed and restored by looking to our elders to continue knowledge through oral tradition and to call on us and our children to be students of our heritage.

We fully realize our work's importance because our citizens are scattered across this country. To ensure tomorrow finds us healthy and secure, we must find ways today to bind a scattered community, providing places for Myaamia people to connect as family and to live our ways. We also accomplish this through modern connectivity, including our quarterly newspaper, websites, and email.

Our nation's leaders recognize that reclamation includes reclaiming our own people, and recognize that our citizens' education must be a Tribal responsibility to ensure that our history, culture, and traditions are accurately conveyed to them.

Our cultural revitalization work is thwarted when our people, especially our children, receive all of their education in the public school system, without input from educators among their people. This led the Miami Business Committee in 1996 to establish annual educational gatherings for language and cultural learning.

The Tribal leadership's economic development efforts have built a national land base with land in five states, providing scholarships, employment for Tribal citizens, language and cultural education efforts, and maintaining the massive infrastructure to maintain it all.

Years ago tribal leaders determined that gaming revenue could be used to establish other, more secure forms of economic development so they created two political economic subdivisions, the Miami Tribe of Oklahoma Business Development Authority (MBDA) and Miami Nation Enterprises (MNE). In addition to owning two casinos and a cineplex in Miami, the tribe has expanded its business operations throughout several states including Kansas, Arkansas, Missouri, Virginia, Ohio and North Carolina.

The Nation now numbers over 4,400 citizens. Our continued existence is due to, and in honor of, those who walked before us, who fought, worked and struggled to remain. In respectful and steely determination, we work to build for our community, provide for and teach our children, and care for our elders. Our economic development is the foundation that allows us to rise to these responsibilities today and continue to support them tomorrow.

We work to assure that while the sun continues to rise, it will shine on the people known as Myaamia.

Tribal members and guests dance late in to the night during the first Stomp Dance on the Tribe's powwow grounds.

ABSENTEE SHAWNEE TRIBE OF OKLAHOMA

Above: Absentee Shawnee Tribe Governor Edwina Butler-Wofle.

The Absentee Shawnee Tribe of Oklahoma currently has 4,131 enrolled tribal members who meet the criteria for enrollment this requires a member to be one-eight or more, as is set forth by the tribal Constitution. The Tribe currently has 16,551.52 acres that are allotted trust land, 595.79 held in trust by the Tribe and 819.53 held in fee status. The Tribe has been known to have lived in the Eastern United States and it is documented that they traveled from Canada to Florida, from the Mississippi River to the East Coast before being removed to the area now occupied. Originally, the Shawnee Indians lived in the northeastern part of the United States in areas now known as the states of Ohio, Indiana, Illinois, Kentucky, Tennessee, Pennsylvania and neighboring states. Treaties in the late 1700s and throughout the 1800s established the Shawnee as having a large population and land holdings in the state of Ohio.

Encroaching colonial settlement persuaded the Shawnees living in Cape Girardeau, Missouri, to negotiate the 1825 treaty with the United States government to cede their lands in Missouri for a reservation in Kansas. However, several years before this treaty was introduced, a group of Shawnees left Missouri to begin a journey south that would lead them towards territory now known as the state of Texas which was under the control of Spain. This group of Shawnees became known as the Absentee Shawnees. The term "Absentee Shawnee" stems from a provisional clause in an 1854 treaty regarding surplus lands in the Kansas Reservation which were set aside for the "absent" Shawnees. The outcome of the Texas-Mexico War (1846-1848) compelled many Absentee Shawnees to leave Texas and move into Indian Territory. It is estimated that the Absentee Shawnees began to settle in Oklahoma around 1839.

In the late 1800s, the Indian agent from the U.S. Government brought soldiers from Fort Reno in western Oklahoma and forced the traditional band of Absentee Shawnees located in Deep Fork River to leave. They were brought south to the area known as Hog Creek and Little River where they were to remain. The group settling here is known as the Big Jim Band. Another band stayed in Pottawatomie County near the town of Shawnee, Oklahoma and is known as the White Turkey Band.

The Absentee Shawnee Tribe of Oklahoma is a federally recognized independent Indian Tribe reorganized under the Authority of the Oklahoma Indian Welfare Act of 1936.

The Absentee Shawnee Tribe of Oklahoma possesses all the inherent powers of sovereignty they held prior to the Constitution of the United States. The inherent right of self-government precedes the United States Constitution, and the governing body of the Absentee Shawnee has never relinquished any part of this sovereign right. Among the power to adopt and operate a form of government of their choosing, to define the conditions of tribal membership, to regulate domestic relations of members, to levy taxes, to regulate property within the jurisdiction of the Tribe, to control the conduct of membership by legislation and to administer justice.

The Absentee Shawnee Tribe of Oklahoma is governed by a constitution. The current form of government evolved over the first half of the twentieth century. This evolution began in 1938 when the current government was formalized under the constitution written to provide statutory authority. The constitution was ratified December 5, 1938, and was amended on August 13, 1988, and was last amended in November 2010.

The tribal government is composed of two separate branches, the judicial branch and the legislative/executive branch. In addition, there is an independent body, the election commission, that's charged with the responsibility of conducting annual elections.

The legislative/executive branch consist of five members: governor, lieutenant governor, secretary, treasurer, and representative, all of whom are elected through referendum elections. This committee has both legislative and executive powers. Each executive committee member is elected to serve a two-year term. The executive committee meets on a monthly basis. It is the executive committee's responsibility to set policy, administer government programs and execute the will of the overall tribal membership.

OKLAHOMA HALL OF FAME

The Oklahoma Hall of Fame, formerly known as the Oklahoma Heritage Association, is a nonprofit organization dedicated to preserving and promoting Oklahoma's incredible story through its people. The organization was founded in 1927 by Anna B. Korn and a distinguished group of prominent Oklahomans to officially celebrate Oklahoma Statehood Day, promote the observance by teachers and pupils with exercises to inspire children with Oklahoma's commonwealth, and create an official ceremony to recognize Oklahomans with the state's highest honor, induction into the Oklahoma Hall of Fame. Programs of the Oklahoma Hall of Fame include history education, publishing, and the Gaylord-Pickens Museum, home of the Oklahoma Hall of Fame.

The Gaylord-Pickens Museum opened to the public on Saturday, May 10, 2007. Located at 1400 Classen Drive in Oklahoma City, this state-of-the-art facility is filled with interactive exhibitory where visitors virtually meet the Oklahomans who have impacted our state, country, and world. The museum is designed to engage visitors of all ages and its garden and event space have become one of Oklahoma City's most desired locations for weddings, receptions, and special events. The museum is open from 9:00 a.m. to 5:00 p.m. Tuesday through Friday and 10:00 a.m. to 5:00 p.m. on Saturday.

The organization sponsors Heritage Week competitions for students in grades three through twelve statewide and offers more than $4,000,000 annually in tuition grants and cash scholarships to high school students. The association has published more than 160 books and is considered the leader in publishing Oklahoma's history. Its Teen Board has raised more than $120,000 since its conception with an annual fundraiser. At the Gaylord-Pickens Museum, the Tulsa World Gallery continues to highlight the artistic talents of Oklahoma, families gather for story time and crafts with Third Thursdays, and people from across the state continue to make their way each year to celebrate statehood at the annual Statehood Day Festival.

Each November, the organization sponsors the Oklahoma Hall of Fame Banquet & Induction Ceremony. Induction into the Oklahoma Hall of Fame is the highest honor an Oklahoman can receive from our state. This black-tie event, televised throughout Oklahoma and surrounding states, is celebrated with attendees from throughout Oklahoma, the nation, and the world.

The Oklahoma Hall of Fame—telling Oklahoma's story through its people.

Above: Guests learning about jazz legend Charlie Christian in the Chickasaw Nation Oklahoma Through Its People Gallery at the Gaylord-Pickens Museum. Christian is one of many Oklahomans celebrated in the museum.

Below: Opened during Oklahoma's Centennial in 2007, the Gaylord-Pickens Museum features exhibits and activities for guests of all ages.

Marketplace/Professionals Financial Services

Oklahoma's retail and commercial establishments offer an impressive variety of choices

SPECIAL THANKS TO

*Frates Insurance &
Risk Management,
Oklahoma City*

*Southwest Trailers,
Oklahoma City and Tulsa*

Express Employment Professionals

Above: Bob Funk, CEO and chairman of the board for Express Employment Professionals.

Right: Bob Funk always wanted to be a rancher. He owns Express Ranches, the No. 1 pure-bred cattle producer in North America.

Below: Bob Funk is named Most Admired CEO.

Oklahoma is a state where the American dream still exists. People with big dreams, much like Bob Funk, can see them come to fruition because of the Oklahoma spirit. This state welcomes entrepreneurs. And, the result is an environment where businesses and employees thrive.

Funk is CEO and chairman of the board for Express Employment Professionals, the largest franchised staffing company, second largest privately held staffing company and the number one industrial staffing company in the United States.

Express provides expertise in evaluation hire, temporary staffing, professional search and human resources, and works across a wide variety of industries for more than 55,000 companies annually.

It all started when Funk moved from Washington to pursue an opportunity in Oklahoma.

"I am an Oklahoman, not by birth, but by choice," Funk said. "For me, coming to Oklahoma was a turning point in my life. I am convinced that no other state would have offered the business opportunities that I experienced as a young entrepreneur. If you want to see your dreams realized, then Oklahoma is the place for you.

"At eighteen, I decided I wanted to be three things simultaneously—a minister, a rancher, and an entrepreneur," Funk said. "When I made that declaration to my boss at the time,

he told me I was dreaming. But, I didn't let that stop me. I worked my way through college and became the first to graduate out of thirty-two cousins. Today, I am so blessed to have seen all three of those dreams come true."

"I became a true entrepreneur in 1983 with the start of Express. My cattle business has been a passion of mine that's led to Express Ranches, located in Yukon, Oklahoma, becoming the number one, pure-bred cattle producer in North America," Funk said. "And most importantly to me, the staffing industry is a ministry because we are able to give hope and encouragement to so many people."

Express has become a powerful economic leader in Oklahoma, in large measure, because of a fearless work ethic of Funk and the employees at the company's international headquarters and thirty-four local franchises. Hard work and determination are part of the Oklahoma culture, and part of the reason that Express has reached its current level of success.

"The 322 individuals at our international headquarters in Oklahoma City and in our offices throughout the state of Oklahoma are the most productive, loyal and driven employees I could possibly ask for," Funk said. "The company is successful because of the relationships we build with employees, potential employees, franchisees, businesses and the community."

Funk aspires to the notion that everyone deserves to experience the satisfaction and self-esteem that comes from being engaged in meaningful work. Whether you are an IT professional, an entrepreneur, a warehouse worker, or any and everything in between, meaningful work can add purpose and fulfillment to your life. It can help shape your

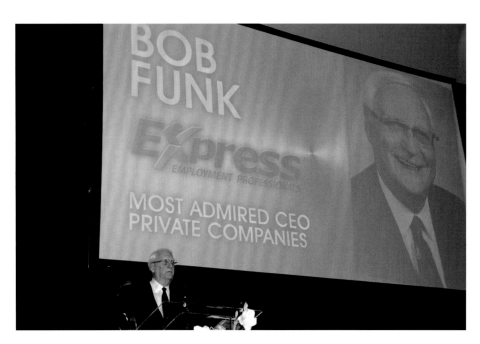

future and the future of your children's lives. Work can add to our satisfaction, success, and happiness. It can give hope.

Former U.S. President Ronald Reagan once said, "The best social program is a job."

"Employment impacts all of our lives. When we help people find a job, it helps restore confidence and provides them hope," Funk said. "A job helps them take care of their family. There is honor and fulfillment in hard work. There is tremendous personal value in a job well done."

Frank Robert Smith is just one example of a job seeker wanting to find a fulfilling career.

With his unemployment running out and money from his retirement package dwindling, Smith was hurting financially. The former Massachusetts drug store assistant manager had lost his job and spent many nights sleeping in his car.

"I had hit rock bottom and was more than ready to make a fresh start at something worthwhile," Smith said. "I was almost out of hope when I went to the public library and used the computer to Google temp agencies. The one that sounded most appealing was Express."

Smith wanted to work and Express found him quite a few job assignments. Because he was not afraid to stock shelves, unload trucks, sweep floors, and rake lawns, Smith showed how determined he was to work hard.

"Express taught me to appreciate the jobs I got and to make the best of each one," Smith said. "Now, when I get jobs that involve a bit more responsibility, I really appreciate them. The jobs have done wonders for my self-confidence."

Above: International headquarters employees support the Thunder during the NBA finals.

Below: Bob Funk and former Oklahoma Governor George Nigh.

Above: Bob Funk welcomes youngsters at Express Ranches, which is home to the famous Express Clydesdales of Express Employment Professionals.

Bottom, left: Throughout the years Express has been a national partner with Children's Miracle Network Hospitals. Here, Bob Funk greets one of the children with CMNH.

Bottom, right: Bob Funk congratulates a scholarship winner at the 2006 Youth Expo.

"We are hope-givers. That's how we think of ourselves," said Rina Donaldson, who has owned the Bozeman, Montana, Express office along with her husband Greg for twenty-five years. "Every day we provide hope for people coming to us, desperate for jobs. Employment is a big deal in people's lives, and when they don't have a job, things can get pretty grim. I've seen it again and again; a job can turn a life around."

Under Funk's leadership, Express has put more than 5 million people to work worldwide and nearly 295,000 in Oklahoma since 1983. "Seeing a person find a job is one of the greatest joys in life," Funk said. "During the past few years, we've put a million people to work. And we have a long-term goal to put a million people to work annually."

The history of Express Employment Professionals began in 1983 with 6 offices in Oklahoma, 2 in Colorado and 1 in Oregon. Express struggled during a time when the oil industry took a devastating downturn. Although local banks and businesses were failing daily, Express managed to keep afloat. That first year, Express Employment Professionals was able to generate gross revenues of more than $2 million despite the depressed economy.

By design, Express offered temporary staffing to help clients and customers through the fourteen percent unemployment recession in Oklahoma. The company marketed probationary hiring as a method of training and "try before you buy" hiring methodology.

And, as an innovator in the staffing industry, Express eliminated applicant fees. To this day, when a job seeker comes to Express, they do not pay any fees. Other large staffing companies have since followed suit in not charging applicant fees.

By 1999 sales for Express topped $1 billion. The franchise network added it 500th office in 2005. In October 2011, Express associates achieved a monumental milestone, working a combined total of 3 million hours in a single week. "To put this into perspective, 3 million hours is equivalent to three more Brooklyn Bridges being built to span New York City's East River or 103 CN Towers being built to preside over the city of Toronto. The likeness of all forty-four U.S. presidents could be carved into Mount Rushmore's granite cliffs twice," Funk said. "And, in just one week,

3,000,000 HOURS WORKED

Express put more than 80,000 people to work at companies across North America and South Africa."

For more than thirty years, this dynamic Oklahoma company has been helping people find work all across North America and South Africa in different trades, industries and professions. From the start, the company's vision has been to help as many people as possible find good jobs by helping as many clients as possible find good people. This is accomplished through a network of more than 700 franchises.

As the number one staffing franchise, Funk not only takes great joy in helping people find employment, but he cannot think of a more rewarding career than helping Express franchisees achieve the dream of owning their own business.

Express began franchising in 1985 because of the lack of available capital at banks. In the first year of franchising, Express experienced phenomenal growth. Within five years, Express Employment Professionals continued with its exceptional growth and was ranked among the top staffing firms in the United States.

"We were determined to grow by finding great franchisees who believed in the Express vision," Funk said. "I have always liked business ownership and I discovered that when you have skin in the game, you play harder, you work smarter and you produce at a higher level."

Franchisees are known for their client satisfaction ratings, achieving Inavero's Best of Staffing Client® Award for five years running and subsequently being Named Best of Staffing® Diamond Award Winner.

Express was recognized as one of the fastest growing privately held companies in the country and named to the *Inc. 500* four years in a row. The staffing giant was named the number one staffing franchise in America for three consecutive years and named one of the top 100 fastest growing franchise systems in America, out of 3,500 franchisors, for two consecutive years by *Entrepreneur Magazine*. In 2014, *Staffing Industry Analysts* named Express as one of the fastest growing major staffing companies and ranked the company number one in industrial staffing.

"The growth we've seen in our company is a testament to the culture of Express," Funk said. "We have an incredible support team that is dedicated to helping people succeed at the franchise level, and our franchisees are personally invested in seeing their communities grow and thrive."

Investing in the community is very important to Express Employment Professionals. They continuously provide support to local and international charities and organizations. And many of the Express owners and their staff members partner with local charities to contribute to causes that are important to their employees and customers.

International headquarters employees at Express Employment Professionals celebrates the company's associates working worldwide for a total of three million hours worked in one week.

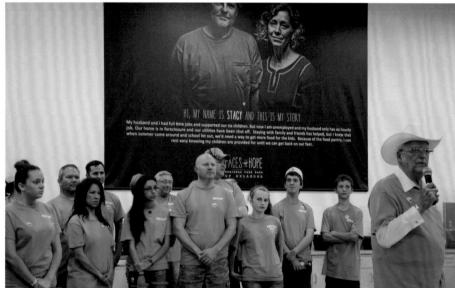

"Giving back is not just a moral obligation for the Express franchise network," Funk said. "We are community driven and our people have a passion to help others. We know we would not be where we are today without the support of the local communities in which our offices are located."

Recognizing that the children of today are the workforce of tomorrow, Express focuses on children as the beneficiary of its corporate contributions. Since 1991—on both a local and corporate level—Express Employment Professionals has contributed more than $4.5 million to Children's Miracle Network Hospitals.

Top and right: Employees from Express Employment Professionals international headquarters and local Oklahoma City offices join together for a day of volunteerism, known as Brand It Blue Day, to give back to the community and help the Regional Food Bank of Oklahoma.

Above: Bob Funk, along with Express Employment Professionals employees, family members and friends, at the Regional Food Bank of Oklahoma.

Beginning in 2013, Express offices from California to North Carolina and Canada come together at local food banks and pantries across North America to help fight hunger—a growing epidemic that impacts millions of people in the United States, Canada, and around the world every day. The company's national day of service, Brand It Blue Day, helps fight hunger through local food drives. In its first year, more than 1,500 volunteers collected food for people in need.

And when devastation hit close to home for the company's international headquarters, Express Employment Professionals donated $300,000 to Central Oklahoma Habitat for Humanity to purchase thirty lots in a Moore neighborhood devastated by the May 2013 tornadoes.

"The May 2013 tornadoes left a deep scar on our state," Funk said. "Following the devastation, the city of Moore and surrounding communities have shown incredible resilience. In every disaster, people need a helping hand. At Express, we are always here to lend that hand."

Express will provide funds every two months for five years toward the purchase of thirty lots. The employment and staffing company will also provide a workforce of its headquarters employees to periodically assist Central Oklahoma Habitat for Humanity with construction. Employees will volunteer for one workday every two months, each time a new lot is purchased.

"More than thirty years after Express was founded, we continue to bring hope to people," Funk said. "I have had the great privilege to be a part of real-life stories where extraordinary men and women saw a big opportunity in even the smallest of jobs. I have seen lives drastically changed by just one job."

Mara Elliott is one such life that has been changed.

Thank you so much for all your help and friendship you and Express extended me during my hardship. When I lost my job after moving to the Kansas City area after two short months, you were there to rescue me. You have a recipe of success from the first phone call I made seeking your help. When I lost my job, your amazing staff embraced me with comfort that everything was going to work out. You gave me courage to keep believing and trusting in my abilities and worth as an employee. The moment I walked into your office, I could sense and feel the values of hope, faith, integrity, and a nonjudgmental attitude coupled with professionalism. Your commitment and dedication to placing veterans and appreciating their service is above and beyond any company I have known.

God bless,
Mara Elliott

Above: A concrete post marking where the historic Chisholm Trail crosses Express Ranches in Yukon, Oklahoma, was dedicated in 1997.

Below: Bob Funk presents a check for $300,000 from Express Employment Professionals to Ann Felton with Habitat for Humanity to help rebuild Moore following the May 2013 tornado. Also pictured is Jennifer Anderson (far right), Express vice president of marketing and communications.

HUCKABAY FAMILY

ALL AMERICA BANK®

Above: T. C. Huckabay, Mountain Park, Oklahoma, 1927.

Below: Left to right, William G. Capps, president; W. W. Runnels, bookkeeper; T. C. Huckabay, assistant cashier; and Marvin H. Clark, cashier, 1927.

Thomas Clayton (T. C.) Huckabay, born on February 28, 1908, in Castor, Louisiana, was the sixth of seven children raised by parents with an elementary school education on a farm. T. C. attended Tyler Commercial College in Tyler, Texas, from 1925-1926. In February of 1927, at the age of nineteen, he landed a job at Planters State Bank in Mountain Park, Oklahoma, as the assistant cashier, bookkeeper, stenographer and janitor paying seventy-five dollars per month. The bank had three other employees, President William G. Capps, Cashier M. H. Clark and Bookeeper W. W. Runnels.

In T. C.'s autobiography he said:

There were two gins in Mountain Park and between them, by running night and day; they could gin about 100 bales of cotton per day. Beginning about October 1st our work load increased to where I spent the time we were open (8:00 am to 4:00 pm) at the window waiting on customers. At that time there were several cotton buyers in Mountain Park and the farmers sold their bales of cotton as soon as they were ginned. After we closed I had to balance my window, get the day's remittance mailed, which required each out-of-town item to be listed, and get them in the mail. After this was finished I did the posting of the checks and deposits. At the height of the season there was a period of about two week that I was 4 days behind with the posting and I was working until 10 and 11 o'clock at night and also Sundays. Cotton was bringing about 26-27 cents per pound and our deposits increased from $80,000 to $380,000 that fall, thus my introduction into the banking business.

The cashier resigned on January 1, 1928, and T. C. was given his position and a raise to $100 per month. T. C. continues:

The years of 1928 and 1929 were considered about normal from a business standpoint. The cotton crops were about the norm, about ½ bale per acre, and the price had fallen to around 20 cents per pound. The year 1930 was extremely dry and the beginning of the Dust Bowl. The cotton yield was very low, the price had dropped to 12 cents per pound, and business was beginning to feel the depression. We made fair cotton yields in 1931 and 1932 but the price had dropped to around 5.75 cents per pound and the depression was nation-wide. Banks were in bad trouble and other commodity prices had fallen along with cotton. Franklin Roosevelt became president in 1933 and declared a bank holiday, closing all of the banks. The sound banks, as diagnosed by the examiners, were allowed to reopen in a week or ten days, with the Federal Deposit Insurance coming into existence. Banks that were in doubt were closed until an examination by the examiners. Our bank was in bad trouble and after the examination we were allowed to re-open under 5 percent

restrictions, which meant for each $100 you had on deposit you were allowed to draw $5 out of the account. New deposits were kept separate and handled under normal conditions. We, of course, lost a lot of business under this arrangement. The closing of the banks occurred in March 1933. In order to reduce the surplus of cotton the government in the summer of 1933 passed a farm bill paying the farmers so much per acre for plowing up a percent of their cotton. A good crop was produced in 1933 and the price that fall rose to about 10 to 11 cents per pound. With the money received from the cotton plowed up, our farm customers got in shape to pay off most of the loans due our bank and were able to get the 5 percent restrictions removed and to obtain FDIC Insurance and to start operating normally again. I might add that during 1933 when we were operating under restrictions our salaries were reduced by the examiners and my salary was $65 per month. 1934 was another dry year and we didn't have a very good year in the bank. 1935 was a very dry year, probably the worst of the years during the Dust Bowl days. On account of attempting to save some cotton he was speculating on that belonged to the bank, Mr. Capps (president of the bank) wrote some checks in early 1935 to keep the Oklahoma Cotton Growers from selling the cotton when the price went down. He did not have the money to pay the checks and on March 25, 1935, he took his life. A few days later the examiners closed the bank.

T. C.'s family has the suicide note left by Capps. It is handwritten on Planters State Bank stationary dated March 18, 1935, and it says,

I take full responsibility for the bank's actions. Huckabay is a good man. He simply obeyed me. He is one of the best and most honest men I ever knew.

Yours truly,
William G. Capps

I do this of my own free will and accord. I am ruined financially. I will shoot myself March 18, 1935.

William G. Capps

T. C. continues:

In order to save my job I worked out a deal with the (Oklahoma) State Banking Department and the FDIC to sell $10,000 in new stock locally and to reopen the bank. I had figured that there was just about enough old capital to take care of the losses in the bank. There was quite a lot of sentiment in Mountain Park to get the bank reopened and I didn't have much trouble in getting the amount of stock subscribed for, but when I contacted the (Oklahoma) State Banking Department that we were ready to go they made the further requirement that we must sell the new stock for $120 instead of $100 so that we would have a surplus of $2,000 in addition to the $10,000 capital. I had more trouble getting the surplus raised than I did the $10,000 capital. I finally talked the prospective stockholders into the additional $2,000 and we got the bank reopened about the 15th of April with me as cashier and the chief executive officer of the bank. I later learned that we were the first bank to be allowed to reorganize and start doing business again since the FDIC had been in existence.

The above was told to Huckabay by a bank examiner.

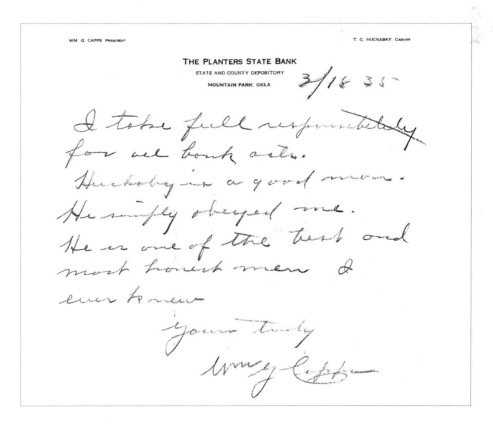

Skipping to 1941 when the United States joined World War II, T. C. continues:

Two men in their early 30's, Joe Krejci and Jerry Cooley, owned control of the First National Bank of Snyder, and in the early part of October 1943, they offered to sell me the bank. I talked to our local draft board and they told me on account of my occupation I was draft exempt. Krejci and Cooley were being drafted into the armed services is why they offered to sell me the bank. At that time the bank had approximately $45,000 in capital, surplus and undivided profit and about $500,000 in deposits. One of their selling points was that the bank might someday have deposits of $1,000,000. I didn't believe it would ever reach that point during my lifetime and I doubt that they believed it either. At the present time (1995) our deposits exceed $26,000.000. They owned slightly over 50 percent of the stock and their price was $39,000. I contacted a friend of mine, Bob Scott of Lawton, who was in the bank stationery and office supply business and we purchased their interest in the bank, each of us sharing equally in the amount of stock bought. It was necessary that I borrow the full amount of the money for my half and I borrowed it from a bank in Wichita Falls pledging my part of the stock, my cattle and land. The deal was completed and I resigned my position at the bank in Mountain Park and become president of the First National Bank of Snyder on November 8th, 1943, at a salary of $250 per month. (T. C. was 35 years old.) About 1 year later I sold my farms, cattle, etc. for enough money to pay for my part of the bank. Approximately 58 months later I purchased Bob Scott's interest in the bank and paid him a nice profit for his interest. We had about a half dozen other people who owned the balance of the bank stock and as the opportunity afforded I purchased all of the stock in the bank. Areta (T. C.'s wife and matriarch of the Huckabay family) and I lived very conservatively for the next few years after buying the first bank stock and moving to Snyder and with our increased income... we began to accumulate some money.

In 1951 I purchased the Planters State Bank in Mountain Park. In 1952 I merged it with the bank in Snyder. In August of 1956, C. L. (Red) Miller, who was Cashier of the bank in Snyder, and I purchased the First National Bank of Sentinel, Oklahoma. At the time of purchase it had about $1,500,000 in deposits. At the time our bank in Snyder had about $1,900,000 in deposits. We gave the owner of the bank $175,000 for 100 percent of the stock and the bank and shared equally on the stock. Red moved to Sentinel to operate the bank. Shortly after the 1st of January 1957, J. W. Brewer, who had loaned Red the purchase price of his stock, requested payment of his loan and I gave Red the purchase price he had paid for the stock plus $10,000 for his stock in the bank. Red resigned his position at the bank and later went to work for the (Oklahoma) State Banking Department.

Business continued to be good during the later part of the 1950s and also during the 1960s and 1970s. Our two banks continued to grow in deposits and the earnings continued to increase with our growth.

The First National Bank of Sentinel and the First National Bank of Snyder converted their charters from national banks to state banks in 1970 and 1971, respectively. First National Bank of Sentinel was renamed Southwest State Bank. The First National Bank of Snyder was renamed Bank of the Wichitas.

In 1975 our executive vice president at the Sentinel bank resigned and Jack Williams, our Snyder bank vice president, took his place. At the time Jack went to Sentinel the deposits of the bank were about $3,860,000 and the capital, surplus and undivided profits totaled about $430,000. At one time Jack had lived and worked in Cordell, which was the county seat of the county in which Sentinel

was located. In the 1980s there was a lot of activity in Washita County in leasing and drilling for natural gas. Quite a lot of the land in the Sentinel and Cordell area leased for $2,500 to $3,000 per acre. The middle 1980s was also the time of many bank failures. All three banks in Cordell were closed as well as several other banks including Carter, Granite and Dill City. On account of conservative operations our bank in Sentinel did not suffer anything more than normal losses during that period. In 1990 the deposits in the Sentinel Bank had grown to $33,756,000 and the surplus, capital and undivided profit accounts had grown to $3,600,000. I attribute the remarkable growth at the Sentinel Bank had during this period to Jack Williams' ability, personality, and the wide acquaintance in the area, the closing of several area banks, the large checks received in the area for the natural gas leases, and the conservative operation of the bank over the years.

Jack Williams still serves on the Board of Directors of Southwest State Bank.

Standing left to right, Wade, Shawn and Gary Huckabay. Seated left to right, T. C. and Todd Huckabay.

Thomas Clayton Huckabay passed away on August 7, 2004, at the age of ninety-six. He worked in the bank in Snyder until two weeks prior to his death. He was a gentleman in every sense of the word. He possessed a gentle spirit, strength of character, a great sense of humor and was abundantly generous and loving. He inspired his family and those around him in countless ways.

Redneck Bank has received national attention. Articles about the bank have appeared in The New York Times, *U.S. Banker, SmartMoney and* The Oklahoman. *Redneck Bank also appears in several college marketing textbooks. In 2008, we created Internet divisions of each community bank. AmericaNet Bank is the Internet division of All America Bank. Redneck Bank is the Internet division of Bank of the Wichitas. Evantage Bank is the Internet division of Southwest State Bank.*

T. C.'s son, Gary Clayton Huckabay, was born on January 3, 1938, in Mountain Park, Oklahoma. After graduating from Snyder High School in 1956 he attended the University of Oklahoma and graduated with a Bachelor of Science degree in Electrical Engineering in 1961. He moved back to Snyder to learn the banking business from his father. In 1969, Gary chartered First Mustang State Bank, a new bank in Mustang, Oklahoma, at the age of thirty-one. First Mustang State Bank changed its name to All America Bank in 1996 upon opening its first branch in Oklahoma City. Gary served as president of All America Bank until 2008 and Chairman of the Board of All America Bank,

Southwest State Bank and Bank of the Wichitas until 2013.

Gary has served the State of Oklahoma with honor in many capacities including being a member of the Oklahoma State Banking Board for twelve years, Oklahoma City Traffic Commission for ten years, Community Bankers Association of Oklahoma (president and Chairman of the Board), Oklahoma Bankers Association of Oklahoma (board member and President's Award), Oklahoma Heritage Association (board member), and Leadership Oklahoma (board member).

Gary has two sons, Clayton Todd (Todd) and Wade Barrett Huckabay, and a daughter, Shawn Huckabay Braden. Todd and Wade attended the Graduate School of Banking in Madison, Wisconsin, from 1992 to 1994, where they were both in the top ten percent of their class. Shawn, Todd, and Wade have served on the Board of Directors of All America Bank, Bank of the Wichitas and Southwest State Bank since 1993.

Todd was born on May 24, 1963. He graduated from Mustang High School in 1981 and attended the University of Oklahoma where he earned a Bachelor of Arts degree in Economics in 1985. Todd worked for a year at First Mustang State Bank, and then moved to Snyder to attend the Huckabay School of Banking, where his grandpa, T. C. Huckabay, taught him how to be a good banker. Todd became president of Bank of the Wichitas in 2005.

Todd has served the State of Oklahoma and his community in various ways including the Oklahoma Department of Transportation (commissioner), Oklahoma Bankers Association (board member), Kiowa County Zoning Commission (board member), Snyder Industrial Authority (president), Snyder Rotary Club (president), Snyder Chamber of Commerce (president), and United Methodist Youth Camps (board member).

Wade was born on February 16, 1965. He graduated from Mustang High School in 1983 and attended the University of Oklahoma where he earned a Bachelor of Arts degree in Finance in 1987. Upon graduation Wade also moved to Snyder to attend the Huckabay School of Banking.

Wade moved back to Mustang in 1988 and worked his way up the chain of command until he became president of All America Bank in 2008.

Wade has served the banking industry and his community in multiple ways including the Banker's Bank Board of Directors, Mustang Area Chamber of Commerce, Oklahoma Heritage Association, United Methodist Church of the Good Shepherd Finance and Endowment Committees, and as director of the Oklahoma Rotarians Task Force. Wade was the director and treasurer of the Rotary District 5750 Foundation, Inc., which was set up for the sole purpose of raising money to replace the YMCA and Federal Daycare Centers following the Oklahoma City bombing on April 19, 1995. The foundation raised over $150,000 for new YMCA Daycare facilities, then revised their goals and raised over $140,000 for tornado victims.

Shawn was born on July 30, 1961. She graduated from Mustang High School in 1979 and attended the University of Oklahoma where she earned a Bachelor of Science degree in Petroleum Engineering in 1983. Shawn worked from 1984 until 2008 for British Petroleum, Park Avenue Exploration, Crosstimbers Oil Company (XTO), and Pinnacle Energy Services, Inc. Shawn joined All America Bank in 2008 as a project manager developing 100 percent

Internet banking divisions for All America Bank, Bank of the Wichitas and Southwest State Bank. Her title is vice president of special projects, which includes websites, marketing, legal matters, oil and gas, remodeling, landscaping, and whatever else needs to be done.

Currently All America Bank, Bank of the Wichitas, and Southwest State Bank have total capital of $11.5M, $10.5M, and $9.5M and total deposits of $118M, $114M, $87M, respectively.

The Huckabays love Oklahoma. Three generations of community bankers and counting....

BANK2

Above: Ross Alan Hill, Founder, president and CEO speaking to the crowd at the bank's tenth anniversary party.

Right: Governor Bill Anoatubby addressing crowd at the bank's tenth anniversary party.

Below: The Bank2 Building located at 909 South Meridian Avenue, Oklahoma City.

Owned entirely by the Chickasaw Nation, Bank2 specializes in making loans to Native Americans from Alaska to Florida and from Hawaii to Maine, and in government-guaranteed business loans, home construction loans and loans to entrepreneurs. The bank was founded in January of 2002 by Ross Alan Hill, president and CEO. Its current individual board members, Brian Gabbard, chairman, Dr. Judy Goforth Parker, vice chair, Ross Hill, James Jennings, Neal McCaleb, and William Paul, were chosen by Chickasaw Nation Governor Bill Anoatubby and approved by the Chickasaw Legislature. Congressman Tom Cole is among the past Bank2 board members of interest.

"Great leaders cast visions which challenge men and women to do far more than they have imagined," states Ross. At a strategic planning meeting held in May of 2001, Governor Anoatubby cast a great vision challenging board members to put the bank on a national footprint, especially to meet the needs of Chickasaws and other Native Americans. The Bank2 charter application was approved within ninety days after 9/11, and in January of 2002, over 400 persons attended the grand opening party.

The bank's Davidson branch was sold in November of that year to allow bank officials to focus their attention on building the Oklahoma City location. The Native American Home Loan Department opened in 2004 to specialize in making HUD-184 Mortgage Loans to Native Americans. That same year, Bank2 received two prestigious honors: the Service Firm of the Year award from the Oklahoma Native American Business Development group and the Small Business of the Year award from the American Indian Chamber of Commerce of Oklahoma.

Many other honors have followed, including being named to the Top 10 Diversified Businesses in Oklahoma (2005-2012); Top 100 Native American Owned Businesses in America (2005-2014); and the Access to Capital Award by the U.S. Department of Commerce Minority Business Development Agency (2011). In 2009, Hawaii Homelands recognized Bank2's efforts for making home ownership dreams come true for Native Hawaiians; and also in 2009 the *American Banking Journal* named Bank2 as the number one community bank in America. It was ranked third in the same category from the *American Banking Journal* in 2010.

In addition, Hill was named a finalist for Most Admired CEO in Oklahoma (2012); and Bank2 was named one of Oklahoma's Top Work Places (2013).

At Bank2's first strategic planning meeting in 2001, Hill asked Governor Anoatubby to share his vision for the bank. "The board had been considering locating the bank in Ada or Ardmore, Oklahoma, and had hoped that it might grow to about $58 million in total assets after about ten years.

"When Governor addressed the board, he cast a huge vision in comparison to that of the board, saying he hoped the bank would have a national footprint," Hill recalls. "Less than eight years later, we had achieved his vision, and had made loans in forty-six states across the country."

Neal McCaleb was steering committee chairman for the bank's formation. When McCaleb was appointed by President Bush in 2001 as Deputy Secretary of the Interior, he had to resign his position with Bank2's formation steering committee. At Governor Anoatubby's request, Tom Cole replaced McCaleb on the board, serving until he was elected to Congress about two years later. McCaleb completed his duties in Washington about the same time, and was named to succeed Cole on the bank's board.

After the board's extensive efforts to find a bank name that could be trademarked, Hill thought of calling it Bank2, though he saw the "2" superscripted. "Each time I showed it to anyone with a math or science background, they read the name as 'Bank Squared,'" he says. "I sure didn't want that as our name, so we made the "2" very, very large and added the line, 'Twice the Bank.' That name met with immediate public acceptance, and now has a national trademark to go along with our national presence. I sometimes get asked if we are part of Bank One or BancFirst, I say, 'No, they are half the bank, we are twice the bank.'"

Because of Bank2's conservative business approach, it actually flourished during the great recession that saw many others reporting large losses. This led to the *American Banking Journal*'s naming Bank2 as one of the top ranking community banks in 2009 and 2010.

"The bank's sixty-three employees care about the customers," Hill says, relating the story of a customer whose cars had to be repossessed when they got behind on their loans. The borrower called to explain that his wife had terminal cancer and could no longer work. The high school-age daughter now had to get up to drive her dad to work, then attend class till lunch, at which time she drove home to help her mother, fix dinner, and pick up her dad at work. She then worked from 6-10 p.m., only to repeat the sequence the next day. When the loan committee recounted this story to bank employees and asked for donations to pay off the family's car loan, employees not only paid the loan, but also bought the family's Thanksgiving dinner, in keeping with the bank's mission statement, "Building Better Lives."

Bank2 sent two employees to help with relief efforts after Hurricane Sandy whipped through New Jersey and New York. These volunteers helped clean mud from houses, prepared and served meals to victims, and again embodied the bank's mission statement.

Employees recently donated over $60,000 to drill water wells in emerging countries after hearing an estimate that 5,000 children under age five die daily from water-borne diseases. Bank2 joined an OKC nonprofit, Water4 to help eradicate this problem by providing safe, clean water. In January of 2014, two Bank2

Above: Helping Native Americans with home loans.

Below: Cleaning mud out of houses in New Jersey after Hurricane Sandy.

Blood Bank, Oklahoma Ethics, and the Oklahoma Native American Chamber of Commerce as well as a score of others.

Bank2, being true to its roots, makes more home loans to Native Americans than any other financial institution in Oklahoma. Additionally, Bank2 has made 4,000 home loans totaling $700 million to members of approximately 250 federally recognized Native American tribes in thirty-seven states. These have included a home loan for an Alaskan native to buy a home above the Arctic Circle.

The bank, which is located at 909 South Meridian in Oklahoma City, has approximately $110 million in total assets, having grown from original assets of just over $5 million to become one of Oklahoma's 100 banks by size. It continues to focus on making home ownership a reality for Native Americans. With a prominent Internet presence, Bank2 has customers across the country who can conduct virtually all of their business on line. This results in lower overhead and much greater geographic diversity, offsetting the weak economy and turbulence in the financial industry.

For more information about Bank2, log on to its website at www.bank2online.com.

Above: Bank2 helping drill water wells in Uganda with Water4.

Bottom, left and right: Helping build Habitat for Humanity homes.

employees went to Uganda to help drill the last water well a village needed to provide sufficient water for inhabitants. These bankers say the experience changed their lives forever.

Other Bank2 projects have included working with the OKC Refuge to re-take one core neighborhood from drug lords and prostitution. The bank has provided loans for young couples to buy homes and move into the area, and has worked closely with the Refuge to help provide financial expertise. The bank's other community and charitable activities include Habitat for Humanity, Oklahoma

Mission360, a Christian-based foundation, founded by Ross Alan Hill, began in January 2010 with headquarters in Edmond, Oklahoma. Designed for the marketplace, it provides services such as teaching CEO's how to use their business for Jesus, mentoring young business leaders, developing growth strategies, business plans and leadership skills based on Christian values. Hill was introduced to the concept on a mission trip to the Dominican Republic in 2009.

Since that time, Hill has traveled the world, conducting business value forums. These forums teach ethical business standards based upon the core values of Christianity. The foundation also provides Christian books to leaders as a secondary source of leadership information. In addition, Hill has written over 1,000 blogs, which are read in 121 countries.

"I could see the need for business leaders to use their influence for Jesus," Hill says. This led him to become involved in numerous overseas mission trips at which he and other executives speak to business leaders and hold breakout sessions.

Believing that the marketplace provides a huge opportunity to reach people for Christianity, Hill has also spoken for CBMC and traveled in Latin America, holding forums on behalf of CBMC. He has also traveled to Colombia and Uganda, where the concept really took root. Hill has since participated in value forums in Ecuador, Guatemala, Kenya, and twice in China.

In a thirteen month period during the development of Mission360, Hill spoke forty-seven times on five continents and throughout the U.S., Oklahoma City area and other Oklahoma sites on Christ's leadership. He has also given away over 2,000 Christian-based books from his executive office at Bank2. His first book, *Broken Pieces—Nothing Is Wasted*, has been warmly received and is available through www.Amazon.com, www.B&N.com and some local bookstores. It was released in Spanish during July and Chinese in October of 2014.

While speaking to about 400 business and communist party leaders at a conference in Beijing, China, Hill told the audience the Christian values used in operating Bank2,

plays a large part in the success of the bank. Bank2 was ranked the number one community bank in the U.S. in 2009 and number three in 2010.

Best-selling author Mark Batterson, stated in his book, *Draw the Circle*, he believed he had never encountered a businessman more devoted than Hill to the cause of Christ. "The bank is his pulpit, and its customers are his congregation," Batterson wrote, adding that Hill "defines business as mission" and is great at both.

For more information, about Mission360 Foundation, go to www.Circle714.com and www.rossalanhill.com.

MISSION360 FOUNDATION

Ross Alan Hill, founder of Mission360 Foundation speaking for the CEO Institute of Dallas, Texas.

AMERICAN FIDELITY ASSURANCE COMPANY

Above: Left to right, C. W., Bill and C. B. Cameron.

Right: Signing incorporation papers.

Personal experience in knowing just how important it is to be able to work and support a family laid the foundation on which American Fidelity Assurance Company (AFA) was built.

The company's founder, C. W. Cameron, was just a teenager when he left school to help provide for his parents and six siblings. This time in C. W.'s life showed firsthand the need for families to protect their income. When his father was injured and could no longer work, C. W. began to appreciate the concept that he later built his career on, "The most important asset any man has is the ability to work and earn a living."

C. W. put that notion to work early in his career. He became a pioneer in offering voluntary supplemental insurance to laborers and then to teachers. During his early years in rural Oklahoma, he would sometimes make sales calls with an associate. Knowing that most potential customers could not take time away from their work in the fields, C. W. demonstrated just how hard he was willing to work to sell a policy by taking the farmer's place working in the cotton fields as his partner explained the importance of insurance to the farmer.

This willingness to do whatever was needed to help his customers earned C. W. a reputation in the industry. By the 1930s, he had become one of the top producers for North American Accident and Health Insurance Company. C. W.'s son, C. B., joined the company in the 1950s and began to work alongside his father. Leadership changes and other factors, coupled with the entrepreneurial vision that C. B. brought to the picture, led to the opportunity for father and son to acquire their block of business and form their own company. They launched American Fidelity Assurance Company in 1960.

C. B. focused much of his attention on the insurance business while C. W. explored his interests in real estate. C. B. led the company in attracting association endorsements, launching annuity sales and then expanding throughout the nation, all while raising a family.

But at the height of their personal and professional success, a 1977 family ski trip brought tragedy to the family. C. B., his wife, their two children and two friends were flying home when their plane crashed into a mountainside. C. B. died in the accident while other family members and friends were severely injured.

Following C. B.'s death, the American Fidelity family rallied to keep the company moving forward. William E. Durrett was named president of AFA. John Rex, CFO and later president, along with Durrett and others in the company, stepped in to fill the gaps left by

C. B.'s death. Both served as company leaders and personal mentors for C. B.'s children, Bill and Lynda Cameron. The AFA family drew even closer during this difficult time.

Not long after the plane crash, Bill headed to Dartmouth for college. After graduation, Bill returned to Oklahoma and began learning more about the family business. C. W. passed away in 1991, and Bill continued to work at American Fidelity alongside William and John to learn more about the company's role in the industry and to understand the founding principles his grandfather and father used to establish the family company.

Bill was named president, chairman of the board and chief executive officer for American Fidelity Assurance Company in 1998. Under Bill's leadership, the company has maintained its values and continued to flourish. The company has grown to become one of the largest private, family-owned life insurance companies in the nation.

Bill's leadership is extended into other ventures as well. He is an active owner and leader of INSURICA, First Fidelity Bank, First Financial Group, Asset Services Company, The Alcott Group, Cameron International and the Tulsa Shock. American Fidelity Assurance Company remains the flagship business of the group.

Based in Oklahoma City, AFA serves more than 1 million customers in forty-nine states. The company has been listed among *FORTUNE* magazine's "100 Best companies to Work For" in America nine times. Since 1982, AFA has consistently been rated "A+" by A.M. Best Company, one of the leading insurance rating services in America.

Throughout its history, the Cameron family has demonstrated an understanding of the need for strong corporate citizens. American Fidelity Assurance Company and its founding family have been staunch supporters of the community. The Camerons, along with William and John, have been instrumental in an array of community initiatives designed to improve the quality of life in the communities where they do business.

Three generations of the Cameron family are at the heart of this company's achievements. Their resilience and unwavering vision enabled them to triumph over professional setbacks and personal tragedy.

"This is a family business, and I like the feeling that I am adding on to the foundation that my grandfather and father built," says Bill. "I am proud of the products and services we sell and the difference we make in people's lives. Reputation means everything."

ChappelWood Financial Services

ChappelWood Financial Services is an independent registered investment advisory firm that has been built on client relationships, reputation, and consistency. The firm prides itself on commitment, creativity, and responsiveness to clients, including efforts to assist clients in cutting operating expenses and taxes while finding the most effective means to achieve goals.

Services include a complete analysis of each client's financial and insurance needs, selection of the most suitable strategist and/or products, and periodic reviews of each portfolio. ChappelWood, celebrating twenty-five years in business, emphasizes education through seminars and their proprietary processes. Highly respected specialists in the field of elder law, tax and trust attorneys are retained to serve as clients' partners to create solutions that meet specific needs.

"Provision of the finest products and investment solutions with premiere and personalized service ensures clients' confidence in our resources for financial advice," says CEO and Chief Investment Advisor Victoria Woods. Woods knows "the open architectural platform with aggregation capabilities is best for our clients, mid-tier millionaires.

"Our mission is to work as a team, continuously striving to improve our performance in order to meet the needs of our clients, employees, suppliers and community. We are the leader in service and relationships. Nobody beats our service. Nobody."

The firm's relationships are with custodians available to the largest banks and warehouses; they have access up to 2,000 researchers that manage $4 trillion in over ninety locations worldwide. With the best and brightest, ChappelWood has achieved a remarkable track record of success providing a team for consistent monitoring. This team "sits on the same side of the table" with the firm's clients, creating personalized investment policy statements.

"An investment portfolio should be based on a complete objective understanding of each client's financial situation and goals, with access to a universe of asset allocation approaches, portfolio strategists, and investment solutions that addresses each client's specific circumstances," Woods explains. "This is exactly what we provide."

In 1989 the operations for ChappelWood began in a spare bedroom in Woods' home. The goals were to grow strategically and build a CFS permanent location. The 1995 bombing in Oklahoma City changed the firm's course to converting a bank building, which changed again with the addition of a new Lowe's and Target in Edmond. These events created the opportunity to envision and found the Financial District of Oklahoma.

Both Woods and the company have earned numerous honors and awards throughout the years. ChappelWood and Woods have contributed actively to community and charitable causes including "Tomorrow's Edmond," the 1995 White House Conference on Small Business, and served as chairperson for the American Heart Association.

Woods is known as The Financial Diva and has written the book, *It's All About the $Money, Honey!* Additional information can be found at www.financialdiva.com; www.chappelwood.com and www.financialdistrictok.com.

Below: Left to right, Victoria Woods with Oklahoma Governor Mary Fallin.

PUCKETT'S FOOD STORES

The story behind Puckett's Food Stores embodies the American Dream. That anyone can succeed and prosper in life through hard work.

In 1884, Jesse Blaine Puckett was born in a half-dugout in Virginia's Blue Ridge Mountains. As the youngest of thirteen children, Jesse was raised by his siblings after losing both his parents before his third birthday. His clothes were handmade from flour sacks and handed down to him. He did not get his first pair of shoes until he was nine years old.

In 1910, Cosley Hill Puckett opened the first Puckett's Food Store in Sayre, Oklahoma. He brought his then twenty-six year old brother Jesse from Virginia to help him run the store. Grocery stores were very different in that era. Farmers hitched their wagons to rings on the store's side wall while bringing in farm fresh eggs and butter to trade for groceries. Apples and potatoes were displayed in bushel baskets and most customers bought a peck at a time. Also, customers brought their own containers to purchase vinegar.

When Jesse was twenty-seven, he married Beulah Kready, a recent graduate of Sayre High School, and used her dowry to purchase the store from his brother. Beulah lost her mother at twelve, leaving her and her sister responsible for their family's cooking and housekeeping. Jesse frequently credited her hard work and thrifty ways for the family's success. This eventually included ownership of thirteen grocery stores in Oklahoma and Texas.

Jesse and Beulah had seven children: Mildred, Jesse Blaine, Jr., Ralph, Marie, Roberta, Calvin, and Arthur. Several of their children, along with other relatives, assisted in the operations of the stores. Everything from carrying groceries for customers and separating truckloads of potatoes to sacking dried beans and fruit.

Jesse eventually owned 10,560 acres in Beckham County and raised mostly Hereford cattle. Some of the chain's 150 employees manned a warehouse. Others worked in a USDA-inspected plant and feed lot near Sayre, where the cattle were fed and slaughtered to provide Puckett's Stores with fresh beef cuts of outstanding quality.

In 1940, Jesse's health began to fail, so he turned over the businesses' management to his eldest sons, Blaine and Ralph. During the Great Depression, Jesse had extended credit to many customers. After learning of his death in 1951, many of the customers to whom Jesse had extended credit to during those difficult times sent checks to the family to settle their bills and offer their condolences.

Today's modern Puckett's Food Stores are owned and operated by members of Ralph Puckett's family.

Jesse Blaine Puckett.

JOHN Q. HAMMONS HOTELS, INC.

Among the city's premier hotels and its only AAA-rated four diamond hotel, Tulsa's Renaissance Hotel and Convention Center, a member of John Q. Hammons Hotels, Inc., is a treasured asset. From its luxuriously appointed guest rooms to well-designed work stations and its award winning Cyprus Grille Restaurant/Merlot's Lounge, the hotel proudly reflects the historic principles of its owner, John Q. Hammons.

In the 1950s, Hammons recognized a growing need for quality hotels throughout the United States. As a successful real estate investor and developer, he had the experience and knowledge required to achieve his lofty ambitions and, in 1958, partnered with Roy Winegardner to purchase ten Holiday Inn Hotel franchises. These properties were immediately successful and served as an early indicator of Hammons' future success in the industry.

The partners went on to found Winegardner and Hammons, Inc., and developed a total of sixty-seven Holiday Inn Hotels. In 1969, Hammons formed an additional company, John Q. Hammons Hotels, Inc., and relied on his own strategies and acumen for site selection. The company's portfolio quickly grew to include Embassy Suites, Marriott, Sheraton and Radisson Hotels as well as several independently branded hotels and resorts.

In 1994, Hammons took his company public and launched a new era of hotel development. Today, the company is once again privately owned, currently operating seventy-eight hotels in twenty-four states.

The Marriott Franchise joined the JQH portfolio in 1996. JQH now manages sixty-five hotels in twenty-three states, with more than 9,000 associates. The portfolio includes 15,000 guest rooms, and 2 million square feet of event space.

Hammons died peacefully on May 26, 2013, at the age of ninety-four. His greatest passions were hotel development and sports, and he remained active in the business until the age of ninety-one.

Over the course of his impressive fifty-two year career in the lodging industry, Hammons developed 210 hotel properties in forty states and was honored with numerous lifetime achievement awards including the ALIS (American Lodging Investment Summit Award), which recognized his contributions to the industry and community.

Today, the company remains headquartered in Springfield, Missouri and is online at www.jqhhotels.com. Its Tulsa Renaissance is devoted to offering traditional service to a contemporary clientele, with gracious accommodations in elegant European style. The hotel, which includes Oklahoma's largest ballroom, is ideally located in the heart of the city's shopping and dining district and surrounded by restaurants, entertainment venues, and Oklahoma's largest shopping mall.

Adhering to the highest standards of hospitality, the Renaissance staff is committed to providing flawless service, extraordinary amenities, and a "bring you back again" experience.

CITY NATIONAL BANK & TRUST

In February 1901 three bankers from Wichita Falls, Texas, stopped for lunch before proceeding to Fort Sill, Oklahoma. The bankers were making the trip to explore possibilities of establishing a bank in the soon-to-be-opened reservation that would become the City of Lawton. The three bankers, William M. MacGregor, William T. Huff and William Keller, were joined by Indian traders, Emmet Cox and George M. Paschal, and the five applied as directors for a bank charter in the new community. The name of the town was not known at that time, but the five assumed it would be named for Fort Sill. The charter issued March 23, 1901, (four months and fifteen days before the opening of the town) bore the name First National Bank of Fort Sill.

In July of that year, the town was named Lawton in honor of Major General Henry W. Lawton and the name of the bank was changed to City National Bank of Lawton. The officers were President George W. Paschal; Vice President William M. MacGregor; and Cashier Frank M. English.

English became president of the bank in 1904 and served for twenty-seven years.

In 1930, J. R. "Dolph" Montgomery and his sisters, Zelda Ferguson and Lena Frensley, bought majority stock in City National Bank of Lawton, a Tulsa holding company, and Montgomery took the position of vice president of City National Bank. English agreed to remain as president for two years but became ill after six months. Montgomery became president at the age of twenty-four in 1931. He was said to be the youngest president of a national bank in the United States.

Today Montgomery's legacy continues into its third generation of bankers, thanks to the leadership of his daughters Roma Lee Porter and Zelda Davis. Both sisters continue to serve on the board of directors for both banks.

Zelda's son, John Davis, serves as president/CEO of Fort Sill National Bank, while Roma Lee's children, George L. Porter III, serves as president/CEO, and Tresea Moses serves as executive vice president for City National Bank.

Left: Original bank, First National Bank of Fort Sill, 1901.

Below: J. R. "Dolph" Montgomery ran the bank for forty-four years.

James M. Larrick Photography

Rose Rock Entertainment

Right: With over two decades of experience in viewing life through the lens of a camera, Photographer James M. Larrick captures a modern view of this emerging state and its people.

OPPOSITE: PHOTO COURTESY OF JAMES M. LARRICK.

James Larrick has been a photographer/ videographer for twenty-five years with a number of years spent in Mississippi, where he worked for several local television stations as well as independently. After the advent of Hurricane Katrina, he returned to his home state where he continues to work in his chosen field.

James says of Oklahoma, "I was born in Norman in the mid-sixties and have the privilege of watching this state transform itself into the prosperous, beautiful place that it is becoming.

"As I drive to every region and capture these images I am astounded by the amount of energy that is being produced in the entire state. When you look closely at our landscape you see the huge impact that energy has on Oklahoma. Wind power, natural gas wells, oil wells, and large high voltage power lines that bind us all together and will carry Oklahoma into the future.

"Our colleges and universities are numerous and all are outstanding. Education options are unlimited. The agriculture department at Oklahoma State is world class. Oklahoma University continues to define itself as a leader in the number of academic scholars it enrolls every year. The smaller schools are just as attractive as options and I am impressed by the beautiful campuses.

"The past few years have brought Oklahoma its first NBA franchise. Bricktown has blossomed into a rewarding destination. I have witnessed the entire downtown area of Oklahoma City transform into a place of great promise and excitement.

"Tulsa remains the center for key oil industry that has supported this state for years.

"With our low cost of living, an outstanding healthcare industry, strong education and a booming energy, Oklahoma is and will remain for many decades to come—a great place to live."

For additional information about James M. Larrick Photography visit www.roserock.us. or call 405-556-1814.

Building a Greater Oklahoma

Oklahoma's real estate developers, construction companies, heavy industries, and manufacturers provide the economic foundation of the region

SPECIAL THANKS TO

Case & Associates,
Tulsa

Disco Automative Hardware,
Sulphur

Jim Leonard Ranch,
Sulphur

Southwest Farm Supply,
Elk City

NORDAM

Top: Ray H. Siegfried II, boxer with a heart of gold.

Above: Ray H. Siegfried II.

Below: NORDAM's original downtown facility.

NORDAM is a family-owned, global aerospace manufacturing and repair firm headquartered in Tulsa, Oklahoma, and employing 2,500 stakeholders across nine facilities on three continents. It is one of the largest independently-owned aerospace companies in the world.

NORDAM originated in the heart and mind of its founder, Ray H. Siegfried II, on April 1, 1969. Ray was a born leader, an entrepreneur and a boxer with a heart of gold. At the age of twenty-six, after earning his degree from Notre Dame and serving in the Army, he went to work for his grandfather's insurance firm in Tulsa. It was a fine job but he wanted something else, a fresh, big challenge that would fully engage his interest and put his massive energy stores to use. While working for the insurance firm, Ray discovered that a tiny operation, for which the insurance firm held a performance bond, was bankrupt. Ray—a newlywed who had tied the knot with wife Milann just six months prior—saw opportunity and envisioned that with a new leader and new owner, the sky was the limit. And soon thereafter, he took control of the company.

The company's name was NORDAM, which was so similar to "Notre Dame" (his beloved alma mater) that Ray felt it must be an omen. After all, NORDAM held six of the nine letters, in the correct order, found in the university's name. So he kept the name, honoring what he saw as providence.

From that point forward, Ray relied on his education, his military background, his sheer inborn optimism and good cheer and Milann's enduring support, to hire the right people—"stakeholders" he called them—and turn NORDAM around, setting the course for its future. Ray and Milann 'raised' their children and their company alike, with family-focused values at the forefront and instilling the golden rule and servant leadership at its core. Throughout his leadership of the company, Ray held fast to his belief that if he hired and brought together the right people, combined with a servant leadership style, the company would soar to great success.

The size of the organization was transformed—largely by Ray's servant leadership and the philosophy instilled in his predecessors—from a handful of employees in Tulsa in 1969 to 2,500 stakeholders worldwide in 2014. For more than thirty years, he served as chairman and the company's chief executive officer, and during this time the firm skyrocketed to global prominence as a leader in aerospace manufacturing and repair and as an employer of choice to thousands of stakeholders around the world. In 2001, Ray was diagnosed with ALS, also known as "Lou Gehrig's Disease." Admirably, he continued to lead NORDAM, assisted by other stakeholders, as the disease progressed. He ultimately relinquished his responsibilities as CEO but retained his chairmanship until his passing in October 2005 at the age of sixty-two.

Now run by the same family for nearly five decades—with Milann continuing to serve on the board—the second generation of Siegfried family leadership continually nurtures and grows the unique culture Ray and Milann established in the beginning, which is based on respect for all individuals, caring for each other, and a healthy dose of fun in the workplace. Today, the company is achieving new heights under the leadership of Ray's daughter, CEO Meredith Siegfried. In addition to Meredith, other Siegfrieds in leadership positions today—all with impressive educational credentials from their Dad's alma mater, Notre Dame—include T. Hastings Siegfried, Bailey J. Siegfried and J. Terrell Siegfried. Raegen Siegfried recently joined the Asia Pacific sales team; he is the son of Ray's brother, Robin—who also helped build NORDAM.

This page: Stakeholders at work.

The Siegfrieds hold firm in Ray's belief that NORDAM was at its beginning—and always will be—what it is because of its stakeholders. In the early 1990s, Ray and Milann had the foresight to ask their kids what they thought was needed for the company to endure from generation to generation. During a family vacation, it was the kids themselves who outlined the family bylaws, which among many other rules includes a list of prerequisites for any second-generation Siegfried wishing to apply for a position at NORDAM: A college degree; at least three years of prior employment with another company; and completion of an employment application, just like any other candidate for any open position. Also, any position applied for by a Siegfried family member must be of equal or lesser responsibility than one currently held at an outside company. Further leveling the playing field, the bylaws require that any career growth a second-generation Siegfried attains within the company must be earned by performance, just as it must be for any other stakeholder. These requirements demonstrate the new generation's respect for the culture of NORDAM stakeholders and ensure the most-qualified individuals—regardless of who they may be—rise to positions of leadership within the company.

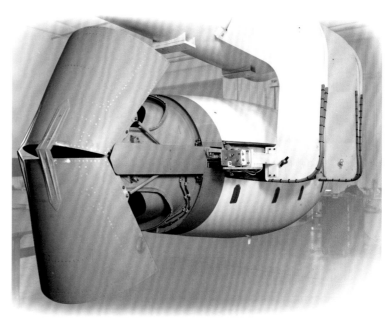

A far cry from the floundering fabrication shop Ray rescued forty-six years ago, today NORDAM engineers composite solutions for aircraft manufacturers, engine manufacturers, and airlines; designs, certifies, and manufactures integrated propulsion systems, nacelles and, thrust reversers for business jets; builds composite aircraft structures, interior shells, custom cabinetry and radomes; and manufactures aircraft transparencies, such as cabin windows, wingtip lens assemblies, flight-deck windows, and simulator screens; and is a major third-party provider of maintenance, repair, and overhaul services to the military, commercial airline and air freight markets. Customers include Aer Lingus, Airbus, Air France, American Airlines/US Airways, Boeing, Bombardier, British Airways, Cessna, China Airlines, Dassault, Delta Air Lines, FedEx, Gulfstream, Pratt & Whitney, Southwest Airlines, UPS, the United States Air Force and Navy, and many others.

Together the Siegfried family and NORDAM stakeholders continue to deliver generous, focused leadership and frontline accountability, a dynamic interplay that has enabled NORDAM to flourish for decades. The company's worldwide reach and its strong standard for leadership remain vibrant as it places a great priority upon community service as overseen by the NORDAM Office of Corporate Responsibility. Through this team,

the company supports the communities where it operates by coordinating involvement in multiple charity organizations, encouraging stakeholder philanthropy and volunteerism. Likewise, NORDAM has long been the presenting sponsor of Tulsa Charity Fight Night—created by Ray and continued by his children—spanning twenty-two years of financial support for Tulsa charities. In 2014 the illustrious black-tie event was reconceived with a new name—Flight Night—a new format with appeal to a wider audience, and a new cause campaign: bolstering the advancement of Tulsa area business, education, and community interests related to science, technology, engineering, and mathematics (STEM) education.

NORDAM's continued success and growth has advanced the Tulsa area through provision of career positions since 1969. The company currently provides some 1,800 Tulsa-area jobs. Stakeholders enjoy a thorough health and wellness program, featuring onsite clinics; financial incentives for routine physicals, dental visits, regular exercise and more; discounted entry fees for area athletic competitions and fitness clubs; and a 'lunch ordering service,' facilitated via the company intranet, wherein stakeholders may order a healthful lunch or dinner delivered to their work locations from a different local restaurant each weekday with no charge for delivery.

Founded upon a dynamic vision and passion for treating people well, NORDAM has also established the Ray Siegfried Leadership Academy (RSLA,) a training ground for any stakeholder identified as a leader. These leadership development sessions are fun and fast-paced. They feature a multitude of educational topics to immerse attendees in the servant leadership model NORDAM embraces, which emphasizes these principles: building on strength, blazing the trail, raising the bar, upending the pyramid, and running to great purpose.

CEO Meredith Siegfried says, "Servant leadership, that's what leadership is. It's making sure that you serve your team. It's ensuring that you create the optimal environment that allows the team to execute—better and better every day. Ultimately, I believe that a positive environment, where people are valued and treated well, is vital for achieving and sustaining success. The upside-down pyramid will yield the results we want: Loyalty and respect, going both ways and all the way around, makes for the strongest team."

She wants every NORDAM stakeholder to feel pride in being part of the company and to enjoy the time they spend here. "I personally look forward to coming to work every day, and I really hope they feel that way, too. Work will always be work, and sometimes really hard work, but I also want it to be comfortable and as much fun as it can be." You will even find Meredith's golden doodle, Lucky Lindy, by her side in meetings. Each Halloween, the family devises a group costume and then embarks upon a day-long tour of every nook and cranny of Tulsa-area NORDAM facilities, distributing candy, admiring spookily-decorated workspaces and stakeholder costumes, and posing for photos. At Christmastime, this fun-loving leadership team again visits all Tulsa locations in a single day, complete with a Santa CEO and jolly contingent of Siegfried elves. Also, each year when the weather turns warm, NORDAM stakeholders and their families can count on a day of NORDAM-sponsored food, family and fun.

NORDAM: Striving to be the premier family-owned aerospace business in the industry.

THE CHARLES MACHINE WORKS, INC.

Above: The Malzahn Bro's. facility.

Below: A 1953 photograph of the blacksmithing shop.

The history of The Charles Machine Works, Inc., manufacturer of Ditch Witch underground construction equipment has its roots in the settlement of one of the last unassigned land areas of the United States.

In 1902, Carl Frederick Malzahn, a German immigrant seeking to escape the harsh winters of Minnesota, moved his family to Perry, Oklahoma, and opened a blacksmith shop with his sons, Charlie and Gus. The business prospered, and several years later, with the advent of an oil boom, it became Charlie's Machine Shop, specializing in repairs for the nearby oil fields.

Young Ed Malzahn, Charlie's son, learned from his elders the process of adapting a business to meet changing demand. In the late 1940s, he began to apply his mechanical engineering degree to a device that he believed would be in great demand once it was produced.

At the time, the process of installing residential utility services—electric, gas, and plumbing lines—involved slow, tedious pick-and-shovel labor. Ed's idea was to create a compact trencher that would dramatically reduce the time and effort of this process. Working together, Ed and his father spent months in the family machine shop creating the prototype of what would be known as the DWP, which stood for Ditch Witch Power.

Ed was only twenty-eight when the first production trencher rolled off the assembly line. It was the first mechanized, compact service-line trencher developed for laying underground water lines between the street main and the house. But it did not merely solve an age-old problem for utility contractors. The DWP paved the way for the creation of the compact trencher industry, which today produces all types of equipment for efficiently installing any type of

underground utilities including water, sewer, and gas lines, and telecommunications, CATV, and fiber-optic cables.

Now known as The Charles Machine Works, Inc., Ed's organization remains a leader in the industry it essentially created. Still based in Perry, Oklahoma, the company designs and manufactures a wide variety of high-quality Ditch Witch underground construction equipment: trenchers, vibratory plows, backhoes, electronic guidance and locating tools, horizontal directional drilling systems, drill pipe, downhole tools, vacuum excavation systems, excavator-tool carriers, mini skid steers and the Zahn® family of power utility equipment. All of these products are recognized around the world for their advanced design, rugged construction, long-term durability, ease of use, and reliability. More information on the product line can be found at www.ditchwitch.com.

Even after achieving household name status in the worldwide construction industry, the Ditch Witch organization remains true to its roots: family and community. Ed has handed over CEO duties to his grand-daughter, Tiffany Sewell-Howard, who represents the fifth generation of the

Malzahn line—beginning with Ed's grandfather, Carl—to run the family company.

The company's extended family includes the residents of and around the town of Perry, population around 5,000. Since the early 1950s, hundreds of Perry-area residents have started and had life-long careers on the expansive campus that contains the company's thirty acre manufacturing plant and training, testing, research and product development facilities. The Ditch Witch plant employs more than 1,300 people. While the temptation is great to reduce manufacturing expenses by exporting those jobs overseas, as many companies have, the Ditch Witch organization is committed to providing American-made products.

Ditch Witch products are an important part of the history of American industry. The Ditch Witch compact trencher has twice been named "one of the 100 best American-made products in the world" by *Fortune* magazine. In 2002, American Society of Mechanical Engineers President Susan H. Kemp awarded the Ditch Witch organization a bronze landmark plaque. More recently, The Travel Channel recognized the company's dedication to homegrown products by featuring the Ditch Witch manufacturing facility on its program, *Made in America*, hosted by John Ratzenberger.

The original Ditch Witch trencher became a permanent part of the new Oklahoma History Center in Oklahoma City in 2005. The trencher's inventor, Ed Malzahn, who was inducted into the Oklahoma Inventors Hall of Fame in 2004, is not exactly ready to be a museum piece. The embodiment of the durability of the machines he pioneered, Ed serves as an inspiration to future generations of innovators.

Above: The original advertisement in the October 1955 Construction Equipment *magazine.*

Below: Ditch Witch RT16 trencher installing a utility in a homeowner's backyard.

GLASS TRUCKING COMPANY

As the Great Depression was moving across the United States, Kansas native Marlin Glass, Sr., set his sights on opening a feed store in Newkirk, Oklahoma. With one truck, Glass Operating Group was born in 1934 and the delivery of feed, chicken and eggs soon became an important mainstay in and around the community.

Above: Marlin Glass' Chevy truck loaded for delivery in 1936.

Below: Ike Glass.

At the onset of World War II, Glass removed himself from the business until the conflict ended in 1945, when he and his family, including his son Marlin "Ike" Glass, Jr., returned to Newkirk to reopen the store. The location of the town itself, which is just south of the Oklahoma/Kansas line, was vital to the family's trucking needs as most of the feed that was delivered came from mills only a few miles away in Arkansas City, Kansas.

As the delivery service flourished, Glass soon decided to begin hauling flour. At the time, bakeries could only receive flour by the bag so Glass helped the Fruehauf Trailer Company design the first ever trailer to transport flour in bulk. Ike, the president of the company today, says, "We've been transporting flour ever since." And it is a history that Ike knows very well.

A 1952 graduate of Newkirk High School and veteran of the United States Navy (1952-1956) serving in the Korean conflict, Ike worked in the family business throughout his college years at Oklahoma State University and received a degree in Personnel Administration in 1961 before returning to Newkirk. It was a particularly difficult period in the history of the company and so Ike went to work for Groendyke Transport and later, Bray Transportation.

While at Groendyke, the company's owner, Harold Groendyke, became a friend and mentor. Ike remembers, "One of his philosophies that has stayed with me all these years is that he never wanted an employee to tell a driver what to do, unless that employee had been a driver at one time."

Ike returned to Glass in 1969, determined to follow the wisdom that Groendyke had so freely shared with him. Today, the majority of Glass employees in operations have come off the road. Ike says, "They know what the customers want and most importantly, they know how to talk to drivers."

As the company flourished into the 1970s and early 1980s, Glass began to diversify its operations and purchased three manufacturing companies to warehouse and distribute the company's products.

The first company, Terra Aqua, is located in Fort Smith, Arkansas, and produces gabions–double twisted, hexagonal woven, galvanized steel mesh compartmented baskets with rectangular box shapes. They offer an environmentally sensitive solution to soil retention slope stabilization and create structures that are naturally free draining.

The second company, located in Maize, Oklahoma, manufactures the fastenings that clip onto the top of steel fence posts, while the third company distributes baking soda as

well as food grade phosphates used in such popular consumer items as prepared corn bread, pancake and biscuit mixes.

Throughout his career, Ike has always believed that the two most important assets for success are good people as employees and an education. He was first appointed as an Oklahoma State Regent by Governor Frank Keating in 1997 and served in the role until 2006. He was reappointed to the post by Governor Brad Henry in 2007 and will serve until the nine year term ends in 2016. "My time as a State Regent has been a very rewarding time for me."

Regent Glass has served as a member of the boards of a variety of organizations in the state, including the Oklahoma State Chamber of Commerce, the Oklahoma Trucking Association, the Oklahoma Heritage Association, the Oklahoma State University National Alumni Association, and RCB Bank and Trust. He has also served as Chairman of the Oklahoma Transportation Center, a joint venture between the University of Oklahoma and Oklahoma State University that unites business, research and education on transport problems in Oklahoma and throughout the nation.

He is a member of the Oklahoma Hall of Fame, Oklahoma State University's Business Hall of Fame in 1998, and the Newkirk High School Hall of Fame.

Regent Glass is active in many civic and community organizations including the American Legion, Navy Leagues, Veterans of Foreign Wars, and Cowboys for Higher Education. Today, Glass Trucking continues its nearly 80 year existence in Oklahoma with $8.5 million in annual revenues, 70 employees, and more than 60 tractor trailer units delivering a variety of goods throughout Oklahoma, Kansas, Texas, Arkansas, Missouri, Louisiana and Nebraska.

Ike and his wife Marybeth have two children, Rob Glass and Jennifer Johnson, two grandsons, Garrison and Jared, and one granddaughter, Ashley.

GHK Company

The Hefner family roots run deep in Oklahoma, from statehood, less than two years after which Judge Robert A. Hefner opened his law practice, founded the oil and gas firm The Hefner Company, and later was Justice of the Supreme Court of Oklahoma; to his son Robert A. Hefner, Jr., who assumed leadership of The Hefner Company, then subsequently formed The Hefner Production Company and drilled many oil wells throughout Oklahoma; to the continuation of the Hefner legacy with his son Robert A. Hefner III, who graduated from the University of Oklahoma in 1957 and founded The GHK Company (www.ghkco.com) in Oklahoma City in 1959. Hefner and privately owned GHK, now celebrating fifty-five years in business in Oklahoma, pioneered deep natural gas exploration in the Anadarko Basin of western Oklahoma, leading the technological innovation necessary to drill and produce the world's deepest and highest pressure natural gas wells, setting many world records along the way.

Robert A. Hefner III, a geologist and geophysicist, proved in the 1960s and 1970s, against all conventional wisdom, that commercial natural gas production in the deep Anadarko Basin was indeed possible. This discovery resulted in major economic and political impact for the state of Oklahoma. Hefner, who remains active today as owner and CEO of GHK, was known as the "Father of Deep Natural Gas" and is considered one of the world's top natural gas wildcatters. His exploration efforts in the Anadarko Basin led to the discovery of several Tcf of natural gas. In addition to setting many world drilling records, in the 1970s GHK initiated and operated the first 3D seismic group shoot in Oklahoma and then became the first operator to successfully use the proppant sintered bauxite in fracturing. In 1980, GHK was the largest leaseholder in the deep Anadarko Basin, owning over 450,000 net acres. Hefner and GHK successfully organized and executed large joint ventures with independent and major oil and gas companies, including, in 1980, the largest on-shore domestic joint venture in the history of the industry with Mobil Oil Corp., resulting in GHK/Mobil interests in over 224 deep wells in Oklahoma's Anadarko Basin and total expenditures in excess of several billion in today's dollars. In the late 1980s, Hefner began analyzing the complex Ouachita fold and thrust belt and in 1997 discovered the Potato Hills Natural Gas Field in the Arkoma Basin in eastern Oklahoma, at the time one of the largest onshore natural gas discoveries in recent decades. Historically, GHK operated about ten percent of Oklahoma's best-producing natural gas wells.

Within the past ten years, Hefner and GHK have returned to Oklahoma's Anadarko Basin, using horizontal drilling and completion technologies to develop tight oil and gas reservoirs, initiating, among other efforts, the Tonkawa horizontal drilling play. Hefner and the GHK Company presently maintain interests in over 100,000 gross acres principally in Oklahoma and Kansas.

Robert A. Hefner III spent many decades speaking widely about his belief in the vast abundance of natural gas in both Oklahoma and the nation and how its expanded use could facilitate economic development to both Oklahoma's and America's advantage. He testified before many U.S. Congressional committees on these subjects, leading to policies enhancing the development of Oklahoma's and America's resources. For over fifty years, he has written and published numerous energy articles and papers, and given many interviews and speeches—to institutions and organizations worldwide—to help keep these issues at the forefront. His groundbreaking book *The Grand Energy Transition* (www.the-get.com) was published by John Wiley & Sons in 2009 and a documentary—*The Grand Energy Transition*—filmed in Oklahoma, was released in 2012. The documentary has been distributed at no charge to raise awareness about the importance of natural gas to the U.S. economy and to provide the facts about the issue of fracking, and can be ordered through the website.

Additionally, to bring worldwide attention to the subject of energy policies and Hefner's thoughts on natural gas abundance, in 2013, China's CITIC Press published the Chinese version of *The Grand Energy Transition* book.

Hefner has been active—over many decades—in numerous philanthropic, artistic and cultural endeavors. In 1980 he donated a building to Ballet Oklahoma for their dance studios and in 1981 won the *Forbes* "Business in the Arts" award. In the mid-1980s he began collecting contemporary Chinese oil paintings from the historic and artistically explosive period following the Cultural Revolution in China and today Hefner and his wife MeiLi continue to develop the world renowned Hefner Collection (www.hefnercollection.com). In 1982, Hefner brought the Phillips Collection—the first major internationally famous collection—to the Oklahoma Museum of Art in Oklahoma City and in 1989 he acquired a large, historic piece of the Berlin Wall, as it was coming down, holding in Oklahoma City, the first of several Berlin Wall exhibitions. In 1997, he brought his Hefner Collection to Norman for an exhibition at the Fred Jones, Jr., Museum at OU. Mr. and Mrs. Hefner have established the Robert and MeiLi Hefner Foundation (www.hefnerfoundation.org), supporting the "Hefner Initiative" program, which currently funds trips to China and Singapore for outstanding students from selected high schools, including the Oklahoma School of Science and Mathematics (OSSM) in Oklahoma City.

Hefner has historically been closely involved with, supported and is a member of many organizations and institutions—statewide, domestically, and internationally. He is a Fellow National in The Explorers Club, a Fellow of the Royal Geographical Society in London, on the International Council at Harvard's Belfer Center for Science and International Affairs, on Singapore's International Advisory Panel on Energy, was a former advisory board member of the International Institute for Applied Systems Analysis in Austria, and is founding director and president of The Bradshaw Foundation (www.bradshawfoundation.com).

During the 1970s and through the 1990s Hefner worked tirelessly for the Oklahoma energy industry and was, variously, chairman of the Oklahoma Energy Advisory Council, chairman of the Independent Gas Producers Committee, on the board of directors of the Oklahoma Petroleum Council, Oklahoma's Representative to the Interstate Oil Compact Commission, on the board of directors of the Mid-Continent Oil & Gas Association, and a founder of the University of Oklahoma Energy Center. Hefner was inducted into the Western Oklahoma Hall of Fame in 1980 and into the Oklahoma Hall of Fame in 2010, where he was preceded by his father, Robert A. Hefner, Jr., (inducted in 1973) and his grandfather, Judge Robert A. Hefner (inducted in 1949). Robert A. Hefner III has 3 children, 7 grandchildren and 4 great-grandchildren—all Oklahomans, with several continuing the family tradition by following him into the energy business.

Above and below: Robert A. Hefner III.

BIO-CIDE INTERNATIONAL, INC.

Above: Bio-Cide's new building, located at 2650 Venture Drive in Norman, Oklahoma.

Below: A section of the Bio-Cide plant.

Bio-Cide International, Inc., is a manufacturer and worldwide seller of antimicrobial and biocidal products based on proprietary chlorine dioxide technology. Their mission is to become a market leader and preferred source for stabilized chlorine dioxide and applications expertise aimed at meeting the needs of industry, consumers and distributors. The company continues to achieve that mission through a commitment to superior products and service, ongoing research and innovation, high ethical standards, and diligence. Bio-Cide distinguishes itself from its competitors by providing "simply the best" stabilized chlorine dioxide products backed by superior applications expertise and service.

Originally founded in 1972 by Bob Danner, Bio-Cide International is the leading manufacturer of antimicrobials that are based on a molecule called chlorine dioxide. These products are considered state-of-the-art newer generation products and provide a higher level of effectiveness with a lower toxicity profile.

The products are environmentally friendly. Once applied and the desired outcome is obtained, the ingredients break down simply into innocuous table salt. The applications range from treatment of food, to being a part of ophthalmic formulations. One of the biggest pharmaceutical companies, Allergan, uses Bio-Cide International products as an important component of their formulations. Bio-Cide International's flagship brands Oxine® and Keeper® are used for the treatment of food, which includes red meat, poultry, seafood and a variety of fruits and vegetables. The company also has an advanced laboratory that employs scientists of varied background, including chemists and microbiologists.

For over thirty-five years, Bio-Cide International has manufactured Oxine and Purogene, proven safe disinfectants effective on a broad spectrum of microorganisms. Located in Norman, Oklahoma, they continue to manufacture a versatile line of chemical disinfectants, sanitizers, deodorizers and preservatives.

Bio-Cide's products are based on the company's proprietary chlorine dioxide solution, which is environmentally safe and effective against a wide variety of microorganisms in short contact times. The products have been tested for quality, effectiveness and toxicity. Bio-Cide has obtained government approvals, licenses and registrations for each product to assure its authenticity and safety.

The initial chlorine dioxide applications were for water treatment, animal health environments, household and agricultural purposes. The success of these products encouraged expansion into larger commercial applications where product approvals have been granted by the Environmental Protection Agency (EPA), the Food and Drug Administration (FDA) and the United States Department of Agriculture (USDA).

Currently, Bio-Cide's products are instrumental in the elimination of microorganisms found in the medical professions, water treatment, food processing plants, dairy and bottling plants, the red meat, poultry and seafood industry, air duct ventilation systems, the oil field industry, and the animal health industry.

The chlorine dioxide based products ultimately break down to simple salt leaving no toxic residues. This allows all of our products to be utilized in conjunction with food products and processing equipment as well as certain specific applications in dental, hospital, and laboratory environments. The technical advances in Bio-Cide's products have resulted in a nearly odorless, clear, stable formula which can be stored, transported and used without special consideration. These properties of the product are pivotal for its new use in oil and gas applications where it is used for the treatment of fracking fluids.

Currently, Bio-Cide has thirty employees in a campus that stretches across four buildings, and its products are being exported to sixteen different countries. For more information about the company, visit www.bio-cide.com.

Above: Bottling line for Oxine product.

Left: Bio-Cide's premium machinist assembling an Airline Water Disinfection System at the Bio-Cide International's machine shop.

R & R ENGINEERING COMPANY, INC.

For almost fifty years, R & R Engineering Company, Inc., has provided outstanding engineering principles and innovative manufacturing designs for the oil, gas, and petrochemical industries. Located in Tulsa County, Oklahoma, the company was founded on July 23, 1968, by Wayne Banes Rumley.

A 1960 graduate of the University of Tulsa, Wayne interned as a rating engineer with Western Supply Company of Tulsa before accepting a position as a process engineer with Champlin Oil Company of Enid, Oklahoma, and later as a rating engineer with ALCO of Houston, Texas.

He returned to Tulsa to start Air Cooled Heat Exchangers in 1963, which he sold in 1968 in order to expand his vision of individualized success in the air-cooled heat exchanger business. Subsequently, Wayne founded his current endeavor R & R Engineering Company, Inc., that same year. Despite having few employees, he was able to provide the engineering and design functions necessary to construct heat exchangers while actively selling his ideas and products to prospective customers. Although the sales trips often involved visiting several states within a twenty-four

Below: Wayne Banes Rumley.

to forty-eight hour time interval, he would return from the long trips eager to oversee the manufacturing of the heat exchangers in his small rented fabrication facility.

In 1971, R & R Engineering expanded onto the company's current site at 12585 East Sixty-First Street in Broken Arrow, Oklahoma. The office and fabrication shop are situated on seventeen acres that was on the outskirts of Tulsa County when the company first began. Although the original office and shop combination was small, necessitating that Wayne and his shop foreman share space with the actual manufacturing process, it was evident that the location would allow for future measured expansion.

Wayne focused on his desire for success. By measuring business cycles and carefully observing the ever-changing financial climate, he prudently invested in R & R's expansion with the goal of adequate growth to meet ongoing demand while remaining debt free. Today, the company includes a large office complex and a modern fabrication facility, totaling more than 50,000 square feet, housing the latest in design innovation and manufacturing programs and equipment.

R & R Engineering Company, Inc., provides equipment to many of the leading oil, gas, and petrochemical firms across the globe. The present team, who share Wayne's visionary approach, are: President and Chief Engineer Tim Childress assisted by the Rumleys; Vice President Warren Burch; Purchasing Agent Warren Benjamin; Engineer Andrea; Controller Beverly Kendrick; Mechanical Engineer Dustin Agee; Sales Manager Nick Parker; Shop Superintendent Jim Hammers; and Heat Transfer Consultant and Professor of Engineering at the University of Tulsa Kraemer Luks. James Cook holds the title of sales manager emeritus. The cornerstone of R & R Engineering's manufacturing capabilities is the dedicated full time shop employees, many of them have been employed here for more than fifteen years.

Wayne functions today as CEO and process engineer of the company with his achievements leading to his inclusion in the University of Tulsa's Engineering and Natural Sciences Hall of Fame in 2004. He has established several chemical engineering

scholarships at his alma mater for students passionate about the field, but required to work during the academic year due to financial demands. In addition, he has established a scholarship in honor of his late wife, Barbara Joan, and his first son, Wayne II, for students pursuing a career in teaching children with special needs. Barbara was an active advocate for the disabled and this family commitment in assisting the disability community has continued through the work of Wayne's daughter, Sharon, who has taught children with special needs for the past twenty-seven years.

Wayne also encourages young adults, currently enrolled in engineering programs at the University of Tulsa, to intern with R & R Engineering and has successfully employed several of the school's graduates at his company. Believing in second chances, the business likewise offers opportunities to those individuals recovering from alcohol and recreational drug use through participation in Oklahoma's Drug and Alcohol Rehabilitation Program (DARP).

Although R & R's reach has expanded throughout the world, the company is proud to still be located in Tulsa County, at its original location on Sixty-First Street. Wayne often consults on air-cooled heat exchanger applications and is recognized as a respected

source on heat transfer issues. Further information about his company can be found online at www.coolersbyrr.com.

HILTI, INC.

In almost anywhere in the world where construction is happening, there will most likely be a distinctive red tool case on the jobsite. That red tool case is a symbol of Hilti: quality people, innovative products and superior services that have been long-standing in the construction industry for more than seventy years.

Hilti North America has a long history in Tulsa, Oklahoma, beginning in 1979. Hilti North America has more than 1,400 highly-trained Hilti account managers and engineers and an additional 1,100 functional employees nationwide.

Incorporating the interests of all the company's stakeholders—customers, suppliers and employees—into its strategy and actively honoring its social and environmental responsibility create the foundation of trust that makes possible the long-term success of the company.

Simply put, the company's mission "to create enthusiastic customers and build a better future" is seen on every front.

With the worldwide headquarters located in Schaan, Principality of Liechtenstein, the Hilti Group is a world-leading manufacturer and supplier of quality, innovative and specialized tools and fastening systems for the construction professional.

Hilti is the only company in the industry with a global direct sales force who make more than 200,000 customer connections every day of the year. They thrive on close customer relationships, where they work together to anticipate and identify customers' needs. That relationship is what drives innovation as they aim to deliver products, services and software that allow their customers to more safely, effectively and productively execute their jobs.

The Hilti Group, under the leadership of Chief Executive Officer Dr. Christoph Loos, operates in more than 120 countries worldwide. It includes manufacturing plants in the United States, Mexico, Europe and Asia, while all research and development functions take place in Liechtenstein, Germany and China.

Founded in 1941, the worldwide Hilti Group evolved from a small family company—including brothers Martin and Eugen Hilti. Initially, Martin and his team manufactured mechanical components and produced commissioned parts and supplies for various industries. Then in 1948, the company began developing an independent product line with the launch of a powder-actuated fastening system. The rest, as they say, is history.

Today, their expertise covers powder and gas actuated fastening, drilling and demolition, diamond coring and cutting, measuring, firestopping, screw fastening, adhesive and mechanical anchoring, and strut and hanger systems as well as dust containment systems.

Hilti's culture is based on the four core values that drive their actions in everything they do:

- Integrity,
- Commitment,
- Teamwork, and
- Courage.

Hilti embraces their mission to "build a better future" for society and the environment, and they live out these values as they work within their local communities. They are encouraged and empowered to find ways to make a positive change with paid time-off to volunteer for nonprofit organizations as well as holding several fundraisers throughout the year for various causes.

In times of disaster, whether in Oklahoma or other locations nationwide, the company springs to action to help their neighbors in need with the donation of tools, gathering of necessities and/or fundraising.

Hilti continues to support more than fifty local, nonprofit organizations such as the American Red Cross, Habitat for Humanity, American Cancer Society and United Way, to name a few.

Hilti, Inc., has been consistently recognized for its outstanding service in the industry and the company continues to uphold a clear value orientation while pursuing a policy of stakeholder value. This focused determination has highlighted Hilti, Inc. as one of the "50 Best Companies to Sell For" by *Selling Power* magazine from 2006 to 2014.

For more information about Hilti, Inc., visit the company online at www.us.hilti.com.

CHARLES D. (CHUCK) MILLS

Chuck Mills of Shawnee, Oklahoma leads by example. He is a successful business owner and executive; a valued civic and community leader; and perhaps most of all, a "practical visionary" for the State of Oklahoma.

As owner and president of Mills Machine Company, Inc., a major custom manufacturer of earth drilling tools founded by his family in 1908, Chuck began his lessons in leadership at a young age, working in the machine shop, alongside his father, David. Chuck began to learn the business, but of equal importance, he gained early insight into the value of practical experience or, "understanding by doing," something that still resonates throughout his private and public career.

Alongside this early work at Mills Machine Company, Chuck's foundation in leadership began with boyhood experiences in scouting, first as a Cub Scout and later as a Boy Scout, where he eventually earned the Eagle Scout Award and where he learned the value of cooperative effort and team achievement.

Through his father's encouragement, Chuck also entered DeMolay, an international organization dedicated to preparing young men for successful, productive lives. It was in DeMolay that Chuck gained more leadership experience and had his first opportunity to make public presentations.

In preparing for these early public performances, Chuck learned not only the importance of careful preparation and scripting, but he began to realize the power of communication. As visual thinker, he recognized the need to translate his thoughts into clear, direct language. As his experience developed, Chuck began to see that the real objective was not simply to share thoughts, but to communicate vision.

Chuck attended the University of Central Oklahoma and earned a BBA in management in 1979. While there he achieved leadership positions in multiple campus organizations including Sigma Tau Gamma (STG) Fraternity and he began a lifelong commitment to this organization and its service-oriented goals. Over the years, he held a variety of volunteer positions, including national president and trustee for the STG Foundation.

Left: Left to right, David and Chuck Mills.

Right: Left to right, Chuck and David Mills.

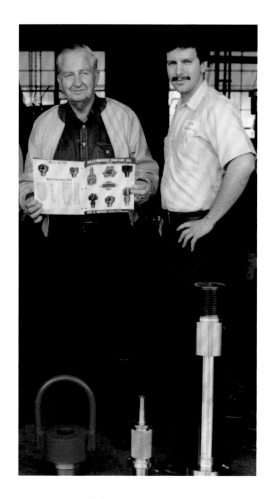

Following graduation, Chuck joined Mills Machine Company, working with his father until David retired and Chuck bought the stock in the company and became president and CEO, a position he has held for more than thirty-five years. Under Chuck's leadership, Mills Machine Company became a multimillion dollar concern that provides a full line of specialty earth boring tools and accessories for water, mining, construction, utility, and environmental applications. Recognizing the emerging opportunities in international commerce, Chuck began to explore foreign markets for Mills Machine Company products. The company now exports an average twenty-five percent of its products to an estimated seventy international markets.

Chuck devotes considerable time to his company, but he also invests a significant amount of time to civic, community and professional organizations. He focuses on leadership positions in four areas including: workforce development and education, global trade, manufacturing and small business. Chuck believes these are all vitally important in the progress and development of Oklahoma.

Among his many state activities, Chuck is currently the chairman for the State Chamber of Oklahoma. He is a member of the executive committee for the Governor's Council for Workforce and Economic Development; co-chair of the OK Workforce Youth Council; and a board member and past chairman of the Governor's International Team, an organization dedicated to a stronger Oklahoma through international trade development. In addition, he is the chairman of the Oklahoma District Export Council, trustee for the Port Authority of the Greater Oklahoma City area, vice chair of the Sauk Business Enterprise Board for the Sac and Fox Nation and a leadership council member for National Federation of Independent Business.

In Shawnee, Chuck served as mayor from 2004 to 2008, describing himself as a business mayor for economic development. Currently, he is a board member of the East Central Workforce Investment Board, Chairman of the St. Gregory's University Business Advisory Committee and a member of the mayor's advisory committee and the Shawnee Chamber of Commerce.

Chuck has been widely recognized for his contributions and achievements in personal, professional and community venues, including: the "Distinguished Alumni Award" from the University of Central Oklahoma in 2012; the Governor's "Small Business Person of the Year" award in 2011; the Oklahoma "Mayor of the Year" award in 2008; and the Shawnee "Citizen of the Year" award in 2006.

When asked about the source of his "practical vision," for doing what he does each day, Chuck points to advice given to him by his father, "Whatever you do, leave things better than you found them." In addition, Chuck is guided by the personal belief that because life is short we should do everything possible to "make a difference" while we can. As he puts it, "We should never have regrets that we could have done more, that we could have helped more people, that we could have made a difference."

Chuck is married to Karen W. Mills and they have two daughters, Britan and Kurstyn.

Chuck Mills.

PELCO STRUCTURAL, LLC

Pelco Structural, LLC, is located on thirty-seven acres in Claremore, Oklahoma. Founded in 2005 by Phil Albert and Phil Parduhn, it borrowed its name from Parduhn's company, Pelco Products, Inc., in Edmond, Oklahoma. "The Pelco Brand is known throughout the country for its commitment to innovation, quality and service and our mission in Claremore was to take that same commitment to the steel pole industry" said Albert, president of Pelco Structural, LLC.

Employing approximately 200 employees and using a state-of-the-art custom manufacturing footprint, the company offers engineering design, manufacturing, and logistics solutions from its 293,000 square foot facility. "Our business model is project-based and specific to our customer's needs" said Albert. "We focus on the design sensitive, delivery critical projects most companies in our market try to avoid." The results speak for themselves. In its first ten years of operation, the company has shipped over $175 million dollars of products in forty-four states and portions of Canada.

The Tulsa Port of Catoosa, Oklahoma, and the availability of galvanizing services in Northeastern Oklahoma figured prominently in the decision to locate in Claremore, Oklahoma. "Our greatest resource is our human resource" said Albert who pointed to the availability of skilled labor in the Rogers County area to grow the Pelco business model. Since opening, the company has been certified by the American Institute of Steel Construction, the American Weld Society, and the Canadian Weld Bureau. Pelco is proud to be "SHARP" certified by the Oklahoma Department of Labor and OSHA since 2011. "SHARP" stands for Safety Health Achievement Recognition Program administered by the State of Oklahoma on behalf of the Federal Occupational Safety and Health Administration. In 2014, Pelco Structural, LLC, was one of only sixteen facilities in the entire state to earn said distinction. Albert credited his stakeholders and their commitment to quality and safety in the workplace for Pelco's earning this very important distinction.

In 2012 the company was selected by the State of Oklahoma as the first recipient of the State of Oklahoma's Excellence in Entrepreneurship Award for growth in jobs and market. In addition, the company has been selected as the 2008 Veterans of Foreign Wars Employer of the Year, Claremore Chamber of Commerce 2009 Business of the Year, and the 2014 Oklahoma State Regents Business Partnership Excellence Award for its partnership with Rogers State University.

Pelco Structural, LLC, is proud to be affiliated with Pelco Products, Inc. and the Parduhn Family in Edmond, Oklahoma.

PELCO PRODUCTS, INC.

Pelco Products, Inc., is an Oklahoma based, family-owned business specializing in the design and manufacture of traffic hardware, utility products, decorative and roadway lighting. With over 150 employees in Edmond alone, it is the largest traffic hardware manufacturer in the nation.

Pelco's founders, the Parduhns, have been involved in the traffic control business for over fifty years. With the invention and success of the Astro-Brac, created in 1968, the company has continued to show a history of innovation and holds many patents. Pelco opened for business in January of 1985 with six employees, all dedicated to manufacturing the most innovative and highest quality traffic hardware. Pelco has grown its product line to include utility hardware, decorative and roadway lighting. Pelco's decorative lighting, street lighting and signage can be seen throughout Edmond, Oklahoma, and in many surrounding neighborhoods and cities throughout the U.S.

The company's original location occupied 2,500 square feet of space near Wilshire and Broadway in Oklahoma City. By 1987, Pelco had expanded into 7,500 square feet with visions of growing more as plans were made to construct a building in Edmond. By the end of its third year, Pelco had grown to twenty-five people. Today, Pelco Products, Inc., of Edmond and affiliate, Pelco Structural, LLC, of Claremore employ nearly 400 in three facilities totaling more than 310,000 square feet on fifty-three acres.

Always at the forefront of technology in its industry, Pelco is constantly providing new products to help customers solve their problems. Pelco's manufacturing technology is world class, utilizing the latest in machining techniques. Employing its own integrated powder coating facility, as well as wet-painting, Pelco is able to provide customized product finishes. The company also adopted the disciplines of Lean Manufacturing in which continuous improvements throughout the organization provides rapid customer response, shortened lead times, and improved product quality.

Pelco has proven to be a pioneer in their industry and has become the standard for products that are superior in design, quality and cost effectiveness. "We sell service and it just happens that we manufacture products that allow us to sell our service."—Steve Parduhn.

ZENERGY, INC

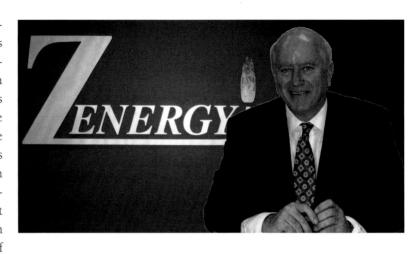

Right and below: Robert M. Zinke.

Zenergy is a Tulsa-based oil and gas exploration and production and midstream company that has grown into one of the industry's most active private oil and gas enterprises. Although the company maintains a low profile, it is presently active in eight states, the Gulf of Mexico, and three provinces in Canada. The company has also operated internationally in the United Kingdom, Portugal, Israel and Nigeria.

The company, formerly known as Zinke and Trumbo, Inc., was founded in 1980 when Robert M. Zinke and David Trumbo met at Hawkins Oil and Gas Company where Trumbo was a geoscientist, and Zinke was vice president of exploration. The two decided to branch out when they saw the need for a quality prospect generation shop with a strategic focus on the mid-continent region of the United States. They actively and successfully explored the mid-continent region establishing numerous field discoveries in Texas, Oklahoma, Kansas and Arkansas throughout the eighties and nineties.

Zinke, the son of a geologic engineer and independent oil and gas operator, often accompanied his father to the oil fields of the Permian Basin as a boy. Zinke's father often tells the story of Zinke as a two year old standing in the dog house of a drilling well in the White Flat Field in Nolan County, Texas, and the tool pusher warning him not to let his youngster drink from the water can or he will be wed to the business forever. Zinke drank from that water can. As Zinke grew into a young man, his father taught him the fundamentals of petroleum geology, geophysics, engineering and exploration economics. Zinke's experience growing up with his father as a mentor was a profound influence that remained throughout his life, education and career. In 1975, he graduated from the University of Oklahoma with a BBA in petroleum land management.

As Zinke and Trumbo developed their company, they gradually found success not only in numerous field discoveries in southwest Kansas, Oklahoma, and the Texas panhandle but also in Utah, Arkansas, the Gulf Coast of Texas, Louisiana, North Dakota and Montana. Zinke believes that Zenergy's success is linked to the ability to adjust. "We've been very adaptive throughout our thirty-five year history, which is probably why we are still in existence and why we've been successful." The company's position in the Bakken Shale oil play of the Williston Basin in Montana, North Dakota and Saskatchewan is a great example. "We initially became involved in the Williston Basin in 1997, so we were definitely one of the early movers and have been one the most active and successful players in the Bakken/Three Forks play. Zinke and Zenergy organized, built and sold two Bakken oil and gas exploration and production partnerships and one midstream entity. A total of approximately $653 million dollars in debt and equity capital were invested in these three efforts and accumulative sales proceeds totaled over $3.1 billion.

Zinke is active in many associations and boards including having served as chairman of the OU Price College Energy Management Board of Advisors and of the OU Price College of Business School Board of Advisors. He also serves as a member of the OU Energy Institute Board of Advisors. He has made several major gifts to the OU Energy Management program funding the Robert M. Zinke Chair for Energy Management and establishing an endowment to support the program and its director.

Zenergy is a proud Oklahoma company that is privileged to currently have in its employ eighty plus Oklahoma energy professionals all who have contributed significantly to its thirty-five year history and success.

ZEECO, INC.

Zeeco is trusted worldwide for the design and manufacture of combustion and environmental solutions for the petroleum refining, petrochemical, production, LNG, biogas, power, and pharmaceutical industries. When founded by John "Jack" Smith Zink on March 22, 1979, as a machine shop, Zeeco focused on the ideals of expertise, innovation, and reliability, which remain the company's foundation of success.

After his departure from the John Zink Company (which was originally founded by Jack's father, John Steele Zink, in 1929 and eventually sold by the family in 1972), Jack purchased a small manufacturing company, known then as Product Manufacturing, which made replacement aircraft parts and component parts for oilfield equipment. When his non-compete clause ran out in the early 1980s, the company, renamed "Zeeco," entered the combustion equipment market, continuing the Zink family tradition that has now lasted for over eighty-five years.

Over thirty-five years and more than twenty global locations later, Zeeco employs over 500 people in its Broken Arrow corporate headquarters alone. The site covers 250 plus acres near Tulsa in a modern facility that includes 73,000 square feet of manufacturing space and the industry's largest research, development and test facilities. Such historic growth has also resulted in a staff of over 1,000 worldwide, with combustion systems and products installed in more than seventy-five countries. International manufacturing capabilities, an engineering brain trust, and next-generation technologies make Zeeco a name trusted by industrial customers worldwide.

Through the years, many of Jack's business and technical acquaintances followed him to Zeeco. Jack hired a broadly talented man named David Surbey who ran the company for many years until his untimely death in 2000, after which Jack named his youngest son, Darton J. Zink, president. The company has grown at an extraordinarily rapid pace under Darton's leadership and direction.

Privately owned, the company remains focused on combustion and environmental systems, by engineering reliable, world-class equipment to meet the strictest emission requirements and survive the harshest operating environments. With its "better by design" philosophy, Zeeco's product development continues to lead the combustion industry.

ZEECO® product lines include ultra-low emission burners, gas and liquid flaring systems, hazardous and non-hazardous waste incinerators, and vapor control solutions. Zeeco has supplied some of the world's most significant combustion systems, including the world's largest multi-point ground flare, largest enclosed flare system, largest elevated flare, and largest acid gas thermal oxidizer. Zeeco has also developed the industry's best performing low and ultra-low NOx burners, installations of which now reduce global pollutants by more than 500,000 tons each year. Moreover, Zeeco designs vapor recovery and control systems that help industrial customers conserve fuel, operate more cleanly and more

efficiently, and quickly recover their equipment investment. With centuries of collective industry experience amongst its employee base, Zeeco has earned a reputation for product innovation, advanced technologies, and superior product reliability with customers that are the world's most recognized names in industry.

Zeeco engineers are constantly researching and improving state-of-the-art technologies, such as flare gas recovery, to minimize pollution emissions from customer plants such as refineries and petrochemical manufacturing. They design cost-effective equipment solutions that help Zeeco's customers meet their regulatory requirements. At the same time, they are always conscious that the dual purposes of environmental preservation and overall plant safety must continue to operate hand-in-glove, as new generations of equipment evolve.

Before Zeeco's new equipment or technology is considered field-worthy, it is thoroughly tested at the company's research, development, and testing facility. Located on Zeeco's corporate headquarters campus, the operation was the first of its kind in the world to be ISO certified. The facility features sixteen full-scale combustion test furnaces and a range of fuels to simulate real-world field conditions. In addition to an incredibly broad scope of burner testing, Zeeco can test and demonstrate flare equipment and incineration systems.

After nearly two decades directing the company, Darton notes, "I enjoy working at Zeeco every day and doubt there's another company quite like it. We are innovative. We are responsive. We are competitive. And, we appreciate the importance of balancing the interests of customers, employees, and community. Zeeco believes equipment integrity can never be overemphasized. That's why our proposed solutions are not necessarily the least expensive. It's also why we work diligently to keep costs as low as possible, while producing quality products that deliver great value. Zeeco's reward? Customers return time and again. Zeeco's flat organizational structure provides an environment where creative brainstorming, problem solving, and idea sharing are encouraged. By eliminating the red tape associated with layers of management, our employees are empowered to make

informed decisions and move projects forward. Doing so optimizes performance. It also makes Zeeco a fresh, exciting place to work. Zeeco definitely is one in a zillion."

Today, the company is headquartered at 22151 East 91st Street in Broken Arrow, Oklahoma, and around the world with offices in Houston, Connecticut, Mexico, Brazil, the United Kingdom, France, Canada, Germany, Italy, Saudi Arabia, Russia, China, Korea, Japan, Poland, Singapore, the UAE, India, and Australia. Visit Zeeco online at www.zeeco.com.

CHESAPEAKE ENERGY

What began as a small company in 1989 has become a leader in domestic oil and natural gas exploration and production. Founded and headquartered in Oklahoma City, Chesapeake Energy Corporation is the second-largest producer of natural gas and the eleventh largest producer of oil and natural gas liquids in the United States. With substantial leasehold in premier U.S. onshore plays, the company explores for and produces hydrocarbons with a focus on responsibility and shareholder return.

Chesapeake is best defined by its core values of integrity and trust, respect, transparency and open communication, commercial focus and change leadership. Introduced by Chief Executive Officer Doug Lawler when he joined the company in 2013, these values serve as both the foundation for company activities and the decision-making framework for the organization.

In complement to its core values, the company operates under a series of business strategies, with careful attention to safety, regulatory compliance and environmental stewardship. These strategies emphasize financial discipline, profitable and efficient growth from captured resources, exploration and business development and drive the company to generate the most value from its operations.

Key to delivering on its business strategies is Chesapeake's commitment to innovation. The company's Oklahoma City campus boasts several facilities that reflect Chesapeake's technical leadership across the industry— leadership that makes the company a more responsible and efficient operator.

Chesapeake's success in unconventional reservoirs starts with accurate and fast core analysis—the study of reservoir rock to determine well conditions. Chesapeake is one of the few operators that has its own "rock lab," the Reservoir Technology Center (RTC). A competitive advantage for the company, the RTC is the industry's most extensive in-house core sample laboratory and also one of the most efficient. Since its opening in 2007, RTC staff members have analyzed more than 60,000 feet of core samples. Using this analysis, geologists can recommend the most profitable areas to drill and develop, helping Chesapeake decrease operational risk and increase its economic rate of return.

Another valuable resource for developing Chesapeake's assets and exploring for new opportunities is the company's 3-D Visualization Room. After capturing seismic data, Chesapeake scientists can recreate 3-D maps of geologic formations beneath the company's leasehold to determine the most profitable locations to drill wells. Dissecting and accurately predicting drilling prospects translates to better land management, well placement and profit margins for the company.

With the analysis complete and drilling plans engineered, Chesapeake's Operations Support Center (OSC) steps in to provide 24/7 monitoring of drilling and production activities. Through a central facility in Oklahoma City, employees can monitor and help direct drilling and geosteering activities. Additionally the facility monitors key production locations and activities. In part due to the targeted work of Chesapeake's OSC employees, the company has significantly decreased its drilling time, while increasing its drilling precision, downhole accuracy and long-term well performance. The OSC also plays a role in the safety of Chesapeake's operations. Not only does the center monitor site progress, OSC employees can also control the site remotely.

Chesapeake is committed to delivering value for its shareholders, providing safe operations for its employees and neighbors and demonstrating technical leadership in the industry. The company is positioned for profitable growth and strong performance while driving for continuous improvement and value generation.

LEWIS MANUFACTURING COMPANY

Right: Lewis Rig housing is custom-designed specifically for rig structures, crows nests, out-buildings or equipment for reliable protection from the elements.

Charles Theodore Lewis, better known as C.T. or "Shang" to his family and close friends, was born March 2, 1907, in Lawrence, Kansas. At the age of five, he traveled with his father and brother in a covered wagon to Payson/Meeker, Oklahoma, while his mother and sisters followed by train. C.T. attended elementary school in Payson and was a 1926 graduate of Meeker High School, where he excelled as a cornet player, a member of the Thespian Club, earning the nickname "Shang Hi Charlie" for his skills on the basketball court, and playing outfielder with another Meeker High graduate and future professional pitcher, Carl Hubbell.

C.T. first developed a passion for flying when he took a short ride on a bi-wing Jenny airplane with a flying performer in the area. The pilot later gave him flying lessons, which C.T. paid for from money he earned while working on area farms. After receiving his pilot's license, he trained young recruits to become pilots in World War II and later bought his own plane and continued to fly for pleasure and for Lewis Manufacturing.

C.T. married Moreane Edmonds in 1925. Upon graduating from Meeker High School, Moreane attended a teacher's college in Colorado and returned to the Meeker area to teach school. Moreane remained in the school system until she moved with C.T. and their children, Charles, Thomas and Mary Frances, to Oklahoma City.

It was a serendipitous event that occurred on an icy February morning that led to the founding of Lewis Manufacturing. At the time, C.T. was working as a derrick man and slipped and fell. He grabbed a nearby drill pipe before sliding to the floor and spraining his ankle. Realizing he could have lost his life or been terribly injured, he decided to make a safety belt and drew out a pattern for an S Model (snap) and B Model (buckle) on a newspaper, which he took to a friend who made the belts for him. When his coworkers began

taking notice of the devices, C.T. made more and began selling them.

After patenting both styles in 1936, C.T. sold them through WECO before founding Lewis Manufacturing in 1947. Originally opened at 705 West Main Street in Meeker, where many items are still manufactured today, the company moved to Southeast Twenty-Ninth Street in Oklahoma City in 1959 before the current location at 3601 South Byers was purchased in 1962 and converted into a main office and additional manufacturing space. In addition to making nine standard designs of the belt today, the company manufactures everything from pulling grips to canvas rig housing for the oil and electric industries and they are sold around the world.

Lewis Manufacturing, LLC is still growing three generations strong after it first began. Indeed, it is proof that "necessity is the mother of invention."

Since its founding in 1966 as a small common carrier with an intrastate permit only to operate in Oklahoma, United Petroleum Transports has become the premier provider of liquid bulk transportation services to energy and chemical industries in the southwest United States.

The company originally operated as Oklahoma Tank Lines, Inc., with Keith Price as owner and president. After deregulation in 1980, Greg Price convinced his dad to purchase a small Pennsylvania carrier and relocate to Oklahoma. This carrier's interstate permit allowed the new company to deliver outside the state under the name of United Petroleum Transports.

After Keith's untimely death in 1993, Greg became president and CEO, a post he still holds. He notes that the company's success is largely due to key relationships developed over the years. Since acquiring Western Commercial in 1997, UPT has expanded its footprint throughout Texas and New Mexico, and in 2002, further expanded to Phoenix at the request of QuikTrip Corporation.

"In its early years Oklahoma Tank Lines handled all convenient store deliveries to local Kerr-McGee gas stations," Greg says. "Then, as the Love's family grew its truck stop network across Oklahoma and the southwest, OTL and UPT grew to meet the rising demand.

"When Love's decided to form its own trucking company, Gemini Transport, UPT transitioned again, this time with customers such as Murphy USA, QuikTrip, OnCue, ConocoPhillips, and many others. UPT prides itself on being flexible and resilient, embracing change and meeting industry challenges," Greg says.

United Petroleum Transports recently moved into the crude industry. Matthew K. Price, vice president of marketing and corporate culture, notes that the company now has more than fifty drivers and equipment hauling crude oil for the nation's largest producers in Oklahoma, New Mexico and Texas.

"Our long-term strategic plan is always to be a resource to our customers, leveraging our relationships to expand offerings to existing and new customers: geographically, products and lanes," Matthew says.

UPT actively participates in several nonprofit groups in Oklahoma City, including Rebuilding Together-OKC, Infant Crisis Services, City Rescue Mission, and Faith Works. The company also plays an active role in all state trucking associations and in the largest industry trade associations the National Tank Truck Carriers and the American Trucking Association. In keeping with Keith's vision, UPT's mission emphasizes safety, customer service, culture, and environment, trusting that success will follow if those goals are met. Vendors, valued customers, and especially the company's professional drivers are all considered part of a lasting legacy, as well as valued members of the family.

UNITED PETROLEUM TRANSPORTS

Left: Keith Price.

MIDWEST FARM SUPPLY

Anyone who complains that big corporations have taken over the country and family-owned and operated businesses are gone can find a prime exception at 220 North Main Street in Elk City, Oklahoma. Midwest Farm Supply, a business with a half-century of history, has changed its name, focus and location several times, but retains a home-town atmosphere that makes shopping a delight. Jimmy and Carol Spieker and their family, who now own Midwest, say it is "just an all-around farm parts store," but customers know that it is much more.

It retains the idea of catering to customers' wants and needs, such as stocking the parts and supplies that will transform frustration into satisfaction when agricultural or lawn equipment needs new mower blades, belts, batteries, or other parts. It is a great relief to know that the needed part can probably be found on a shelf right in their hometown. That is a comforting feeling when the grass keeps growing or weeds are overtaking the garden while the mower or tiller sits idle. If a part is not in stock, the helpful people at Midwest Supply are likely to ask if this is a recurring problem, and to order an extra supply of that part to be on hand for the next breakdown.

In August of 1963, Jimmy Spieker started his career at Herring Equipment, a forerunner of Midwest Farm Supply, while Carol began work there in early 1987. The Spiekers bought part interest in the business in 1985 and became its sole owners in 1999. They had previously bought the Allison Building to use as a warehouse, and later moved their store there.

When their son, Cory, graduated from Oklahoma State University, he returned home to work in the family business. During this era he had many job descriptions, helping wherever needed, including driving the delivery truck across the country to pick up new equipment. Jimmy and Carol's daughter, Jeanna Casebeer, a Southwest Oklahoma State University graduate, joined the family at Midwest after working at several accounting jobs in Oklahoma City. The Spiekers are now the proud grandparents of Catelynn Celeste, Chelsea Marie, Clancie Helen and Cassidy Jordan (C. J.) Spieker, and of Jessica Rhae and Kobi Brennan Casebeer.

Despite sales fluctuations in the 1980s, the introduction of new lawnmower models, along with climbing oil and gas production spurred 1990s sales. A top product "package" during this era was a compact tractor with trailer, loader, cutter and box blade. These were popular with weekend farmers and for odd jobs around larger farms.

In 1993 the Spiekers dedicated one building to a Farm and Garden Shop, selling John Deere lawnmowers and hand-held equipment. They also expanded their Stihl line from basic chainsaws to more hand-held products. They were notified in January 2009 that they would no longer be a John Deere dealership as of June 1. Learning that Western Equipment was not going to open an Elk City store, the couple decided to close their 807 South Main site and move to 220 North Main to operate a farm, lawn and garden parts store. Employees Ted Duerr, Steve Wilson and Melanie Herndon remained with Midwest; Jenna took a year off but is now back in the accounting office; and Cory is working in the oilfield.

"We made a lot of changes at that point." Carol said. "Now we sell used agricultural and lawn/garden equipment, portable compressors, generators, space heaters and all kinds of farm-related products. In fact, Midwest has just about anything for lawn and garden work, including frequently needed parts for tractors and equipment."

Both Carol and Jimmy have lived in Elk City most of their lives, and have many lifelong friends in the area. If they do not have the parts a customer needs, they will order any that are still available, Carol adding, "If we can save them a 60 to 100 mile drive, we certainly will."

Midwest Farm Supply is located on the opposite corner of the block from the retired Parker Drilling Rig. "It's easy to find when you come into town from the east," Carol said. "We're only a half block off 3rd Street or Business I-40, which is the old Route 66."

Family members are involved in a variety of church activities and other community activities. Carol and Jeanna work with Relay for Life. Jeanna is the co-chair of that group and Carol is the Survivors' chairman. This year's Relay for Life goal is $60,000 to $70,000.

BANNER CO-OPERATIVE ELEVATOR ASSOCIATION

With a history dating back almost a century, the Banner Co-Operative Elevator Association was formed to serve farmers who wanted to create their own marketplace for their products. It was incorporated on March 30, 1920, under the laws of the State of Oklahoma, to operate at Banner, Canadian County, Oklahoma, where its main office is still located. Less than a month later, the association bought its first elevator from the Yukon Mill & Grain Co.

Located at 4175 North Banner Road, El Reno, Oklahoma, this farmer-owned grain elevator and farm supply cooperative also sells feed, fuel and fertilizer, including dry, liquid and NH3.

Members of the first board of directors included B. O. Finley, Karl Bornemann, H. H. Maxey, W. S. Barnes, all of Banner; and J. L. Newland of El Reno. Minutes of the board meetings during the association's early history note that coffee and ice cream would be served at the annual meetings, with one person always designated to get the ice cream.

During its ninety-four years of operation, the association's activities have been directed by eight managers: Mr. Hayes, Bud White, Alvin White, Harry Youngblood, Larry Loomis, George Christie, Gene Sokolosky, and the current manager, Gerald D. Kammerer.

Both membership and financial worth of the co-op have grown through the years. In 1927, it bought a building formerly used as a garage to be transformed for use as a John Deere implement warehouse. More land was purchased in the 1950s, and a new concrete elevator was built. In the latter part of that decade, the association added an annex, increasing its capacity to 348,000 bushels.

Further growth occurred on October 19, 1964, when an adjoining twenty acre tract of land was purchased from R.L. and Stella Henry. A portion of that property located south of the concrete elevator became the site of a new warehouse in 1967. In the years that followed, a dry fertilizer blend house was added, along with more warehouse space and steel bins, bringing the capacity at that time to 1,030,000 bushels and a seed cleaner.

In June of 2002 the Banner Co-Op purchased the facility at Union City, Oklahoma, from Terminal Grain, Kenneth Miles. This raised the storage capacity to 1,492,000 bushels.

From a single employee in its earliest years, the number has increased to twelve full-time and five part-time workers, and sales recorded by the Co-Op have reached $16 million. Current board members are James M. Parizek, Paul Hurst, Ray Bornemann, Dennis Elmenhorst, Ken Carel, Charles Kolar and David Siegrist.

Hammer Construction was originally founded by Jack Hammer in the 1950s, providing roustabout labor to companies in south central Oklahoma. Considering Jack Hammer's fragile health in the late 1980s and the daughter's desire to preserve the thirty year old family business, Shirley took on the small enterprise at a time when oil and gas service opportunity was minimal, at best. Facing the overwhelming challenges created for the industry by the fatal fall of Penn Square Bank, Hammer searched for an 'earth moving' opportunity. Opportunity was revealed when Hammer built Chesapeake Energy's very first drilling pad site in Garvin County, Oklahoma. In spite of an ever changing market, Hammer has enjoyed twenty-five continuous years of service to Chesapeake. Targeting the active Barnett Shale play in 2001, Hammer entered north central Texas as a woman-owned new-comer. The company has forged lasting relationships with independents and major energy entities by providing timely and quality services. Remaining true to its roots, Hammer continues to provide heavy equipment and personnel to build pad sites, pits, roads, and skilled labor crews for production equipment installation and maintenance. The portfolio has evolved to include compressor and facility work, midstream services, a commercial site prep department, and several niche services, such as rock crushing, hydro-excavation, and wood debris disposal that support the special needs of Hammer's clients.

Hammer Construction, Inc., and its leadership have been awarded special recognition as a top quality, competitive provider of services in every market it serves. The CEO often jests to her team "to keep air in the tires" to facilitate the ever emerging energy hot spots. That statement has led Hammer to work in Pennsylvania, West Virginia, Louisiana, Kansas, Texas, and of course, the home base of Oklahoma. With a corporate office in Norman, Oklahoma and field locations in Weatherford, Lindsay, Elk City and Kingfisher, Oklahoma; Bridgeport, Texas; and Hugoton, Kansas, Hammer's 250 employees accept projects ranging from day work to $3 million projects.

Hammer Construction is a second generation, woman-owned, private entity led by Shirley Hammer and her family, Taylor Jennings and Robby Moore. Equipped with legacy leadership and a dedicated team, Hammer crews proudly join thousands of oil fields hands making energy history again and again.

Above: Left to right, Taylor Jennings, Shirley Hammer and Robby Moore.

Below: The Lindsay Operation.

SPONSORS

ABOUT THE PHOTOGRAPHER

JAMES LARRICK

James Larrick has been a photographer/videographer for twenty-five years with a number of years spent in Mississippi, where he worked for several local television stations as well as independently. After the advent of Hurricane Katrina, he returned to his home state where he continues to work in his chosen field.

James says of Oklahoma, "I was born in Norman in the mid-sixties and have the privilege of watching this state transform itself into the prosperous, beautiful place that it is becoming.

"As I drive to every region and capture these images I am astounded by the amount of energy that is being produced in the entire state. When you look closely at our landscape you see the huge impact that energy has on Oklahoma. Wind power, natural gas wells, oil wells, and large high voltage power lines that bind us all together and will carry Oklahoma into the future.

"Our colleges and universities are numerous and all are outstanding. Education options are unlimited. The agriculture department at Oklahoma State is world class. Oklahoma University continues to define itself as a leader in the number of academic scholars it enrolls every year. The smaller schools are just as attractive as options and I am impressed by the beautiful campuses.

"The past few years have brought Oklahoma its first NBA franchise. Bricktown has blossomed into a rewarding destination. I have witnessed the entire downtown area of Oklahoma City transform into a place of great promise and excitement.

"With our low cost of living, an outstanding healthcare industry, strong education and a booming energy, Oklahoma is and will remain for many decades to come—a great place to live."

For additional information about James M. Larrick Photography visit www.roserock.us. or call 405-556-1814.

About the Authors

BOB BURKE

Bob Burke has written more historical non-fiction books than anyone else in history. His 112 books are all about Oklahoma's incredible heritage. Born in Broken Bow, Oklahoma, he was the director of a large state agency in Governor David Boren's administration and managed Boren's first campaign for the United States Senate. He is a graduate of the University of Oklahoma and Oklahoma City University School of Law. He is the father of Robert, Amy, and Cody, stepfather of Natalie, Lauren, and Calli, and grandfather of Nathan, Jon, Ridge, Fallon, Greyson, Mia, and Emerson. He and his wife Chimene live in Oklahoma City where he practices law and writes books.

ERIC DABNEY

Eric was born and raised in Kremlin, Oklahoma, and received his undergraduate and graduate degrees from the University of Central Oklahoma, where he now serves as an adjunct professor in the College of Education. He is the series editor for Bob Burke's Commonwealth Publishing, is a contributing writer of over thirty publications of Lammert Inc.'s Historic Publishing Network, and is the co-author of *Fearless Flight: The Adventures of Wiley Post*, *Historic South Carolina*, *Historic Rogers County*, and *The Life of Bill Paul*. Eric and his wife have three daughters and live near Guthrie, Oklahoma.

PHOTOGRAPH COURTESY OF ALICIA MOORE PHOTOGRAPHY.

For more information about the following publications or about publishing your own book,
please call HPNbooks at 800-749-9790 or visit www.hpnbooks.com.